The Politics of Scarcity
Water in the Middle East

Published in cooperation with the
Center for Strategic and International Studies,
Washington, D.C.

The Politics of Scarcity

Water in the Middle East

EDITED BY

Joyce R. Starr and Daniel C. Stoll

Westview Press
BOULDER & LONDON

Westview Special Studies on the Middle East

Copyright © 1988 by the Center for Strategic and International
Studies

Published in 1988 in the United States of America by Westview Press,
Inc., 5500 Central Avenue, Boulder, Colorado 80301, and in the United
Kingdom by Westview Press, 13 Brunswick Centre, London WC1N 1AF,
England

Library of Congress Cataloging-in-Publication Data
The Politics of scarcity : water in the Middle East / edited by Joyce
R. Starr and Daniel C. Stoll.
     p. cm. -- (Westview special studies on the Middle East)
  Bibliography: p.
  Includes index.
  ISBN 0-8133-7285-2
  1. Water supply--Middle East. 2. Water supply--Political aspects--
Middle East. 3. Water resources development--Middle East.
4. United States--Relations--Middle East. 5. Middle East--
Relations--United States. 6. Middle East--Strategic aspects.
I. Starr, Joyce. II. Stoll, Daniel C. III. Series.
HD1698.M53P65 1987
333.91'00956--dc19   87-29548
                                                            CIP

Printed and bound in the United States of America

6   5   4   3   2   1

Contents

Foreword

As a policy studies institute, the Center for Strategic and International Studies conducts research that is both timely and anticipatory.

The water policy research project, initiated by Joyce R. Starr and Daniel C. Stoll of our Near East Studies Program, is a prime example of this focus. Their effort, a major project entitled "U.S. Foreign Policy on Water Resources in the Middle East," concentrated on the impact that emerging water problems in the Middle East will have on U.S. strategic interests in the region. In the process, they brought together an extraordinarily varied body of water experts, representing the academic, governmental, and business communities in both the United States and Middle East.

This book is the culmination of more than fifteen months of research, interviews, and conferences. Given the scope and depth of its treatment of pertinent issues, it should become an invaluable study for students of the Middle East as well as for seasoned analysts.

Amos A. Jordan
President Emeritus,
Holder of the Henry A. Kissinger chair
in National Security Policy, and vice
chairman of the Board of Trustees
Center for Strategic and
International Studies

Preface

The Middle East stands at the precipice of another major natural resource crisis. Before the twenty-first century, the struggle over limited and threatened water resources could sunder already fragile ties among regional states and lead to unprecedented upheaval within the area.

In July 1986, the Near East Studies Program of the Center for Strategic and International Studies (CSIS) launched a fifteen-month research effort on the U.S. government response to the unfolding crisis, "U.S. Foreign Policy on Water Resources in the Middle East." Our goal was to recommend a strategy for the future that could protect and reinforce U.S. interests.

Our intended audience was the U.S. policymaking community, specifically those agencies and divisions in the executive branch involved in water-related diplomacy, development, and data collection. The study focused on the region's three major river basins: the Jordan, the Tigris/Euphrates, and the Nile. We concentrated on those countries or areas in the region facing severe water shortages and declining levels of water quality: Egypt, Jordan, Iraq, Israel, the West Bank and Gaza Strip, Syria, and Turkey.

The perspective of the Middle East players themselves was essential, and thus experts from the region were brought in to critique our ideas as they took shape. A steering committee of U.S. experts from wide-ranging disciplines provided intellectual direction.

As the project unfolded, officials from U.S. government agencies participated, generously sharing their time and views. We were impressed by the dedication and professionalism of these experts. Although increasingly restricted by reduced funding and constraints within the government, their skill and far-sightedness have shaped programs that stand as a source of pride for our nation.

There was consensus among the participating experts that diplomatic momentum should be encouraged wherever possible. The group stressed, however, that diplomacy per se is a long-range, laborious, and usually tortuous process. By contrast, technical advances--although not a substitute for diplomacy--can result in discernible, near-term gains.

U.S. government and private sector representatives participating in this effort recommended that the U.S. government concentrate on four policy areas:

* Development of advanced water technologies
* Encouragement of more efficient resources management and conservation strategies
* Improvement in coordination among U.S. water agencies
* Attention to long-range research and planning

These goals could be met through structural and programmatic changes at minimal cost and with high returns. Congressional awareness of the looming Middle East water resources crisis and support for a strengthened U.S. government position is essential.

Specific recommendations for action include:

1. The creation of a coordinating body within the U.S. government for all Middle East water research and development programs. This interagency group would serve as a data clearinghouse and "institutional memory" for the government's work on water issues.
2. The creation of a U.S./Middle East water program to encourage the development of

advanced water technologies. Topics of study would cover a wide range of technical issues, including: horticulture, genetic research and development, pollution control, water reuse strategies, and the application of solar energy to water technologies. Special emphasis on research related to desert regions would have applications for both the Middle East and the U.S. Southwest.

At present, the United States is the only country in the world capable of exerting leadership on water resource development and cooperation in the Middle East. We have the capability to forge ahead. What is required at this juncture is the vision to persevere.

Joyce R. Starr
Director

Daniel C. Stoll
Research Associate

Near East Studies Program
Center for Strategic and
International Studies

Acknowledgments

The production of this volume has left us deeply indebted to many friends who served as guides, counselors, and mentors.

His Excellency Boutros Boutros Ghali, a man of great foresight, merits special appreciation as the individual who planted the conceptual seed from which the entire project took root. The generous support of Prince Charitable Trusts—and the great personal interest of William Wood Prince—enabled us to translate our dreams into reality.

Without Sy Taubenblatt's continuous support and vast knowledge, the project might not have materialized. Ralph Katrosh's intellectual vigor guided us through the ordeal of adapting our findings to the framework of readable prose.

Although we did not discover Steven Lintner until after the project's inception, he proved to be a stalwart friend who dedicated invaluable time and inspiration to our cause. Prolonged and positive encouragement from M. Peter McPherson, Lieutenant General E. R. Heiberg, III, and Mike Van Dusen—members of our Steering Group—convinced us that we were doing something right. Other members of the Steering Group contributing their time and expertise included: T. Louis Austin, Edward Azar, Richard Fairbanks, Senator Charles Percy, John E. Priest, James R. Sharpe, Senator Paul Simon, and Joseph Sisco.

At the Center for Strategic and International Studies, we wish to thank former President Amos Jordan for his willingness to grapple with elusive ideas and his efforts to bring this project to fruition as a major CSIS undertaking. Additional thanks go to a host of supporting CSIS actors, including: David Dakake, Scott Doberstein, Seth Levy, Kenneth Libre, Margo Paz, Joshua Soven and Alison Withey.

We are also indebted to the ground breaking work of such experts as John Waterbury of Princeton University and Thomas Naff from the University of Pennsylvania.

Finally, we are grateful to all U.S. and Middle Eastern experts from both the public and private sectors who gave so generously of their time and specialized knowledge. Particular appreciation goes to those overworked specialists within the U.S. government who responded to our ideas with genuine interest and concern.

J.R.S.
D.C.S.

The Politics of Scarcity
Water in the Middle East

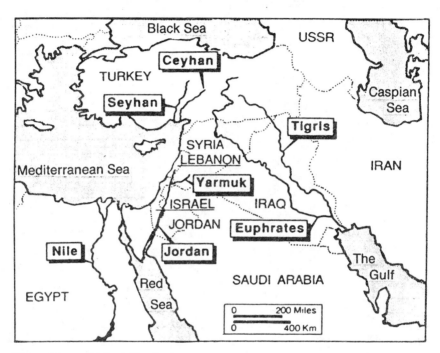

Where risks are highest: The fresh-water supply is a major issue throughout the Middle East, but the outlook for Egypt, Israel, Jordan, the West Bank, the Gaza Strip, Syria, and Iraq is particularly grim. Almost all major water resources are shared by more than one nation, heightening the potential for conflict. (Map courtesy The Financial Times of London © 1988)

1

Water:
The Next Strategic Resource

Ewan W. Anderson

I am making a way in the desert and streams in the wasteland...to give drink to my people....
--Isaiah 43: 19-20

    Resource geopolitics in the Middle East has been long dominated by one liquid--oil. However, another liquid, water, is now recognized as the fundamental political weapon in the region. Despite the expected growth in Western dependence upon Gulf oil toward the end of this century, we can safely predict that water will increasingly shape the politics of the area. Throughout most of the Middle East, rainfall varies from about 250mm to 400mm per annum with none at all in the extensive desert areas. The only areas in which falls of 1000mm a year or more are recorded are the higher mountains of Lebanon, the Maghreb, and restricted areas of Turkey and Iran. For agriculture, insufficient rainfall is, of course, a major problem because cultivation requires at least 400mm; areas with less than 250mm can only be used for rough grazing. Comparatively high rates of population growth throughout the region make the need for increased economic development, particularly in agriculture and industry, obvious. Thus, it is vital to utilize all available natural supplies of fresh water and also to develop new sources. Throughout the Middle East, all the governments concerned are giving high priority to water policy; investing in water exploration, construction of barrages of various kinds, and development of alternative supplies, particularly through desalination.

Financial measures, however, cannot by any means provide a total panacea. For example, the lower the total rainfall the more unreliable the rainfall becomes, so that years of drought may be followed by catastrophic floods. Procedures, therefore, need to be geared to extracting every possible drop of water, while (under different conditions) preventing massive losses into the sea. Costly recharge dams may stand idle for two or three years and, in the fourth, prove totally inadequate. Another problem, resulting from both high evaporation rates and the meticulous use and reuse of water, is the enhancement of dissolved mineral content, which leads to increasing salinity of the soil. Because this condition can only be effectively cured by flushing with fresh water, it is not surprising that in many areas of marginal physical conditions and poor management practices, soil deterioration is marked.

Many other hydrologic and economic difficulties could be discussed, but there are two, essentially political, aspects of the Middle East water crisis that should be identified. First, with regard to natural occurrences, the boundaries of water supply sources, both surface and subsurface, may not coincide with political boundaries. Such situations can lead to competition or even conflict. Perhaps less obvious, however, is the fact that abstraction on one side of the boundary may seriously affect supplies on the other. In the Middle East there are several cases of such disputes, both actual and impending. The second aspect, both political and strategic, concerns the nature of water infrastructure, and more particularly, the reliance upon artificial sources of supply. Many states have become dependent upon a few major installations that, in the event of hostilities, could be relatively easily damaged.

Table 1.1 reveals the full extent of the water crisis by showing the projected increase in population and decrease in water availability by the year 2000. As the minimum ideal is 1,000 m^3 per capita per annum, there will obviously be a shortfall, in many cases marked, in most countries of the Middle East.[1]

NATURAL RESOURCES

With the sole exception of the Nile, all the perennial rivers of the Middle East are to the north of latitude 30°N, and even beyond that parallel there are considerable areas with only ephemeral surface flow. Therefore, the opportunities for barrage construction are limited; but the majority of perennial rivers have one dam, although multiple damming is becoming the norm. Major multipurpose dams can, of course, exercise a great influence on development downstream, which can be particularly important when the lower reaches of the river are in a different state. For example, the Ataturk Dam on the Turkish section of the Euphrates (to be completed by about 1991 with a capacity to irrigate approximately 750,000 hectares) must affect the various schemes in Syria and Iraq. Although at least thirty-five major dam schemes are projected for the permanent rivers of the region, the most marked tendency is toward constructions on seasonal water courses. In some cases these may impound sufficient water to form a permanent reservoir, but in most they are designed to check losses and increase recharge into the subterranean aquifers. There are plans for sixty such dams of varying sizes to be completed in Saudi Arabia by 1990.

Throughout the Middle East, groundwater has been a major (and in many cases the key) source of supply for millennia. Water is commonly obtained from springs and wells, but in Iran and the eastern Arabian Peninsula (notably Oman) subterranean canals known as qanats or aflaj have been crucial. Because of the dramatic increases in water requirements since the 1950s, great strain has been placed upon these sources. This applies particularly to those countries that have the greatest reliance upon ground water, notably Israel, Libya, and the Gulf states. Thus, almost half of the Oman Agriculture Ministry's budget allocation for water in the second plan has been set aside for the maintenance and repair of aflaj.[2] Overpumping of shallow aquifers leads inevitably to a fall in the water table; the drying up of wells, springs, and subterranean

3

canals; and often (as a result) the forced migration of the population. Furthermore, such water-level depletion often permits the incursion of saline water from the coast as landward water pressure decreases. In this way, the fresh water supplies of Bahrain have been totally destroyed. Even in the Batinah, the most important agricultural area of Oman, there are marked increases in salinity along the coastal fringe. Thus, schemes for aquifer recharge are under active consideration in many countries, particularly Oman.

Another possible measure is the use of the deep "fossil water" aquifers, although these are considered by many to constitute a nonrenewable resource. The most spectacular example is the investment by Libya of over $3.3 billion in the Great Manmade River Project to irrigate some 180,000 hectares. When complete, the river will stretch from Kufra in the southern Fezzan to the coast and will facilitate agricultural and industrial development around most of the shoreline of the Gulf of Sirte.[3] At least in the medium term, however, this must be viewed as only a temporary solution.

With both surface and ground fresh water resources either unavailable or approaching exhaustion in many areas, great urgency is attached to the search for alternative sources. Chief among these alternatives has been desalination. More money has been spent on installations in the Middle East than in any other part of the world. Indeed, the region possesses over 35 percent of the world's desalination plants and over 65 percent of the total desalting capacity. Nonetheless, the costs of production by conventional means are between $1 and $2 per cubic meter ($m^3$) of water. Great efforts have been made to reduce these costs, particularly through the use of solar power. Extensive research has been conducted at the Kuwait Institute of Scientific Research, and accelerated developments may be expected once the sophisticated new Qatar Solar Energy Research Station has been completed. At present, the most promising method, and one that could be replicated on a small scale, is that of the saline solar pond in which the sun's radiated energy can be collected and stored.[4] Depending on the scale, operations costs could be reduced to between three-quarters and one-third of those incurred by conventional desalination plants.

The second most important alternative source, but one limited to irrigation, is reprocessed sewage. Water from this source is already in use in many countries, notably Jordan and Qatar, and in Kuwait there are plans to irrigate up to 16,000 hectares in this way. As there seem to be no Islamic objections to this method, its use appears likely to expand over the coming years. A further solution, often discussed but rarely fully costed, is the regular import of water. The well-known and dramatic possibility of towing icebergs from the Antarctic seems feasible, but practicalities such as the control of melting and the distribution of water have not been addressed.

A further suggestion and one that has already been implemented to a certain extent is for water to be imported by tanker. In particular, France, Japan, and the United Kingdom (each with well-placed regions of surplus and well-established shipping infrastructure) have been trying to develop this idea. Already Gibraltar and Malta receive regular supplies, and last year Spain imported large quantities of water from France. There are, however, major problems of logistics and strategic vulnerability, if not of actual costs. Long-term reliance upon a foreign source for such a vital commodity as water seems, to say the least, unwise. This concern applies also to the possible development of international water pipelines within the region.

WATER GEOPOLITICS

The most obvious and pressing geopolitical problems, both actual and potential, are those involving the distribution of surface water. In any situation in which a catchment is divided between a number of states there is the possibility of conflict. Because upstream abstraction will affect the quantity and quality of water available to users downstream, unless the flow is sufficient for all needs throughout the year, some agreement about sharing is required. Control, however, remains in the hands of the upstream state, and thus politically motivated actions can never be entirely discounted.

In the Middle East there are three such shared major basins, each of which exhibits a potential for conflict over water. The Nile catchment is shared by a number of countries, but only four--Uganda, Ethiopia, Sudan, and Egypt--are in a position to exercise significant influence hydrologically. Egypt alone is a sufficiently developed user to be considered a water crisis country.

Less stable in political relationships is the basin of the Tigris-Euphrates and Shatt al-Arab, a region divided principally between Turkey, Syria, and Iraq. All three countries are undergoing rapid development, and, from their expenditure on major water projects, it is clear that all appreciate water's future crucial role. The third catchment, that of the Jordan, is by far the smallest but is also the most volatile in international relationships. The key riparian states are Israel, Jordan, and Syria, although in the case of Syria, developments on the Euphrates have a higher priority. This is the one basin in which water piracy has actually been seriously contemplated. Such purely political activity results from the fact that boundaries in the basin divide not only the individual states but Arab nations of contrasting political persuasions and, more important, the Arab world as a whole from Israel.

Two other rivers of geopolitical significance are the Orontes, which flows through Lebanon, Syria, and Turkey, and the Litani, the whole course of which is technically in Lebanon. There have been no disputes over the water of the Orontes, but the Litani flows in its lower course through Israeli-occupied territory and has been the subject of much speculation. Thus, a seventh country, Lebanon, emerges as one with a key role in Middle Eastern water geopolitics.

In Turkey, Iran, and the Maghreb there is additional surface flow, and major hydraulic schemes have been implemented. There are no obvious sources of conflict. In the case of the

Maghreb countries, the political boundaries tend to parallel the directions of flow, and thus there is little opportunity for disagreement. Apart from the major catchments of the Tigris and Euphrates, the catchments of Asiatic Turkey that flow to the Black Sea and to the Mediterranean are basically self-contained. Furthermore, flow to the Black Sea is such that a scheme to transfer water across the watershed into the Tigris-Euphrates basin has been suggested. Economic, technological, and, particularly, ecological objections, however, have been so strong that there is virtually no possibility of such a major scheme being implemented. Iran includes within its borders some of the minor headwaters of the Tigris, but these are mainly in restricted valleys and as a result, dam building seems most unlikely. The remainder of the Middle East (Libya and the Arabian Peninsula) has very little surface flow, and therefore political disputes over water are likely to take a different form.

The Basin of the Jordan

The most intractable water problems are in the basin of the Jordan. Not only is it a small river, but the countries involved, with the exception of Lebanon, all face major water shortages. The river is a complex system with varying hydrological characteristics among its contributing basins. They vary not only in total volume but also in reliability. The most important source of the upper Jordan is the Dan Spring, which contributes some 50 percent of the discharge. The upper Jordan itself accounts for approximately 40 percent of Israel's water budget. The other major contribution to the Jordan is from the Yarmuk River.[5] It is significant that only 3 percent of the area of the Jordan basin lies within the boundaries of pre-1967 Israel. After the various extractions, the total discharge to the Dead Sea is equivalent to about 2 percent of the annual flow of the Nile, or 7 percent of the Euphrates in Syria. Despite these limitations, however, it provides approximately 60 percent of the water for Israel and 75 percent of that for Jordan.

The major development in Israel was the construction of the National Water Carrier, completed in 1964. It lies entirely within Israel's pre-1967 boundaries and takes water from the northern edge of Lake Tiberias, along the coastal plain to the Negev Desert. There are contributions from other sources to the flow, which averages 320 million cubic meters (MCM) per year. On a smaller scale, the Huleh marshes in northern Israel have been drained. The other major project was the Mediterranean-Dead Sea Canal, anticipated to have an annual flow of 725 MCM, but plans for this have now been shelved. Other options in Israel include the greater use of groundwater. There is evidence that such projects in the south of the country have been successful. An increased program of desalination has also been considered. More cost-effective, however, is recycling from sewage. Because the cost of artificial sources is high, it is clear that Israel, within its present boundaries, will always have major water problems.

While Israel was implementing its early schemes, Jordan was involved in cooperative efforts with Syria in initiating the Great Yarmuk Project. A major part of this project, the upper East Ghor Canal, was completed in 1964 and further expansions have occurred subsequently. Nonetheless, the canal has not yet reached the Dead Sea, as originally planned. Jordanian plans to construct the Maqarin Dam on the Yarmuk to help alleviate its problems have been opposed by both Syria, where the river rises, and by Israel, which fears the effect of water loss.

The West Bank and to a certain extent the Golan Heights are increasingly vital to the water economy of Israel. Apart from direct abstraction, recharge drawn off within Israel occurs over the West Bank. The Israeli presence on the Golan Heights guards against any possible diversions in the upper Jordan valley.

The West Bank has become critical as a source of water for Israel, and it could be argued that this consideration outweighs other political and strategic factors. There are three major aquifers in this area. Before 1967, Israel was exploiting two of these almost to the maximum by pumping from within its own borders. After 1967, Israeli control of the West Bank allowed access to the eastern aquifer, with an estimated yield of 66 MCM annually. The growth of Jewish settlements in the West Bank has increased the water requirement, but there is a major disagreement about the actual amount available. Although Israel considers the area to be self-sufficient, Jordan is convinced that there is a large surplus for use within Israel itself. Suffice it to say that Israel's use of water on the West Bank is controversial. One result has been the limitation of Arab agricultural development. Deep drilling has resulted, in some cases, in the desiccation of Arab springs and wells. Although the data cannot be checked, it has been asserted by some authorities that the increase in water consumption by Israel since 1967 has only been possible because of territorial expansion.

Despite the completion of six reservoirs, Israel has gained comparatively little for its water budget directly from its occupation of the Golan Heights. Most water required in the area is taken from Lake Tiberias, and supplies for the remainder of the country are thereby depleted. The Israeli presence in southern Lebanon, however, has brought control of all the sources of the upper Jordan. It has also given rise to Arab fears that Israel may try to divert the waters of the Litani into the Hasbani River through a tunnel, thereby providing Israel with an additional 500 MCM of water annually.

The Jordan basin is clearly well suited to integrated development, but all schemes proposed so far have failed, as a result of the extreme enmity between the Arabs and Israel. Probably most significant was the scheme proposed by Eric Johnston, appointed by President Eisenhower to be a special ambassador and charged with designing a comprehensive plan for the Jordan system. The starting point was the Main Plan, which included a number of dams on the various tributaries; the reclamation of the Huleh marshes; and gravity flow canals down both sides of the Jordan Valley. Subsequent modifications were put forward, each apportioning different allocations to the riparians Lebanon, Syria, Jordan, and Israel. Finally, the Johnston, or Unified, Plan received general acceptance, although it was not ultimately ratified by the Arab League Council. Nonetheless, the proposed allocation of water (Jordan, 52 percent; Israel, 36 percent; Syria, 9 percent; and Lebanon, 3 percent) has been retained by all states as a guideline in the implementation of their own schemes. Thus, despite the failure to develop a multilateral approach, the Johnston Plan was more successful than any other proposed development in the Jordan basin.

Although there have been constant disputes over water within the region, some of these tensions have led to substantial geopolitical threats. An Arab summit meeting in 1964 resolving to divert the headwaters of the Jordan tributaries outside Israel, as well as Syria's subsequent diversion attempts, resulted in a number of large-scale border clashes. The outcome of these schemes would have brought about the diversion of water from the Hasbani, Dan, and Baniyas to the Yarmuk. Thus, the water conflict has effectively been militarized, and in 1969 Israeli raids on the East Ghor Canal resulted in severe damage. Furthermore, damage occurring as a consequence of war, together with population movements, have severely set back the agriculture program in Jordan.

Thus, the Jordan River has been the scene of more severe international conflicts over water than the other two systems of the Middle East, and it remains by far the most likely flashpoint for the future. Not only has tension remained high, but, more important, the water situation, particularly in Israel and Jordan, has continued to deteriorate. Indeed, it is estimated that Israel currently consumes approximately 95 percent of all possible supplies. With the development of both states so crucially tied to water, it is only to be expected that further disputes and even conflict will result.

The Basin of the Tigris-Euphrates

The Tigris-Euphrates system is the only basin
of the three where there is a marked surplus of
water, but owing to present and future
developments, there are actual and latent
geopolitical problems. Unlike the main Jordan
River riparian states, neither Turkey, Syria, nor
Iraq is facing an imminent water shortage.
Instead, these countries face problems of
management, apportionment, and development
planning, which are leading to disagreement among
the riparian states. Tensions may also escalate,
given the extensive irrigation and hydroelectric
power projects in hand.

The Euphrates basin covers an area of 444,000
km^2 and includes surface tributaries, wadis, and
areas of purely subsurface recharge. It is
divided between Turkey (28 percent), Syria (17
percent), Iraq (40 percent), and--as a source of
wadi flow and subsurface contributions only--Saudi
Arabia (15 percent). The overall measured
contributions of both Iraq and Saudi Arabia,
however, are extremely small and the mean annual
low is effectively generated within Turkey (88
percent) and Syria (12 percent).[6] The Tigris is
more restricted in area, partly as a result of the
capture of much of its head waters by the
Euphrates. It receives flow from a number of
important left bank tributaries, however, most
notably the Kharun, a major river in its own
right, furnishing the main proportion of the
Iranian input.

Both rivers are subject to major fluctuations
in flow, both seasonally and also year to year.
Thus, although one function of upstream dam
building, water abstraction, may lead to disputes,
another, that of discharge control, is beneficial.
The mean annual discharge of the Euphrates is
approximately 32,000 MCM per year, that of the
Tigris 42,000 MCM per year, and that of the Kharun
20,000 MCM per year. All three carry
comparatively large amounts of sediment, often
excessive in the case of the Tigris and the
Kharun, and all suffer large losses from
evaporation during the summer months. Because the
three key states, unlike those involved in the

11

Jordan basin apportionment, are aligned geographically in linear fashion, water quality is of great significance. Water draining back after irrigation will tend to have an enhanced salinity, particularly given the high rates of evaporation in the region.

The area that is now modern Iraq, has been concerned with irrigation projects since antiquity. It was also the first of the three riparians to begin major construction with the Hindiya barrage, completed in 1913. There have been several other such schemes, and it is estimated that almost 50 percent of Iraq's agricultural area is under irrigation. Indeed, Iraq is considered to be the one Middle Eastern country to be self-sufficient in agriculture, based on irrigation.[7]

Immediately upstream, Syria is also a fast-growing economy, dependent to a large degree upon agriculture. Initial exploitation was concentrated upon the Orontes, but then attention turned to the Euphrates, as the Tigris forms only one short section of the border. The major construction on the Euphrates was the Ath-Thawrah project for both hydroelectricity and irrigation. It was expected that the resulting irrigated region would total from 200,000 to 500,000 hectares, but so far this has not been achieved. There are also schemes for the Khabur, but all the Syrian projects are behind schedule.

Turkey has development projects for both the Euphrates and the Tigris, but so far the accent has been upon the former. The first completed scheme was the Keban Dam, finished in 1973. Because the lake behind the dam was filling at the same time as that of the Ath-Thawrah Dam in Syria, the temporary effect on flow was significant. Indeed, in examining possible sources of dispute, the sequence of project completion dates needs careful scrutiny. Too many coincidences would obviously lead to dramatic depletions in discharge over a short period and would be unacceptable to downstream riparians.

Of the other major schemes, either planned or under construction, by far the most important is the Ataturk Dam, which will require some 10,000 MCM of water annually and will, it is hoped, irrigate as much as 700,000 additional hectares. If this abstraction is added to the 7,000 MCM projected for Syrian plans, and allowance is made for the additional evaporation resulting from the large lake surfaces, the amount of water in the Euphrates entering Iraq would be reduced from 30,000 MCM to 11,000 MCM per annum. With its own schemes, Iraq claims that its future minimum requirements will be at least 13,000 MCM. The major upstream projects, however, are lagging well behind their scheduled completion dates and, given the current economic positions of both Turkey and Syria, it is possible that some of the larger schemes may not be completed in the foreseeable future.

In addition, apart from other sources, such as groundwater and recycling, Iraq could make greater use of the discharge in the Tigris. In fact, the Tharthar Canal project, which at the moment diverts Tigris water into the Tharthar Depression and thus controls flooding, is planned to be extended to the Euphrates. This would facilitate the transfer of flow from one river to the other. The water budget would be affected adversely, however, if the agreement signed between Iraq and Jordan for piping water from the Euphrates to Jordan, were to be implemented. Apart from the engineering problems, the implementation of such a program would do little for the Iraqi case when water apportionment is discussed with the other two riparians.

The only documented crisis over water in the basin occurred between Syria and Iraq in 1974, when the effect of new Syrian and Turkish dams reduced flow in the Euphrates to approximately 25 percent of the normal flow. Various threats were issued, including a threat to bomb the Ath-Thawrah Dam, and troops were amassed along the frontier. Following the intervention of Saudi Arabia, however, Syria agreed to release additional water from the Ath-Thawrah Dam in June 1975. Nevertheless, this was not an incident concerned simply with water, as there had been tension between the two regimes for some time.

Although so far there have been no political agreements, in 1984 Syria called for the establishment of a multinational Euphrates River

Authority and for a joint meeting to discuss riparian rights.[8] Thus, due to current planning there could be severe shortages in the basin within the next four to five years, the possibility of actual conflict seems unlikely. Although their political orientations vary, the three governments concerned appear to have evolved a reasonably stable working relationship.

The Shatt al-Arab, produced by the confluence of the Euphrates and the Tigris, as well as discharge from the Kharun, presents rather different problems. The lower part of the river provides the border between Iran and Iraq and is involved in frontier rather than water issues. During the long history of the dispute, few practical problems concerning water have ever arisen. Still, aerial photographs published in 1987 showing defensive canals constructed by Iraq to impede Iranian military progress have changed the picture. Should upstream abstraction sufficiently lower the flow of the Euphrates, these defensive moats would dry out and their effectiveness would be considerably diminished.

The Basin of the Nile

The Nile River is unique in several respects. It is the longest river system in the world and drains approximately 10 percent of Africa. More important, no river system flows through so many different climatic regions, and as a result, none has such a complex hydrological regime. In this respect, there is a major contrast between the main stream, the White Nile, and its two major tributaries, the Blue Nile and the Atbara. Also of great significance is the fact that from its confluence with the Atbara to the Mediterranean, a distance of 1,800km, the Nile has no perennial tributaries.

With a fast-growing population, at present numbering 51 million and virtually all settled in the Nile Valley, Egypt's need to increase the agricultural area is paramount. Therefore, water demands only increase, and the sole supply of any importance is the Nile itself. Progress is being made with recycling and also with locating fresh

14

sources of groundwater, but as yet these have yielded comparatively modest amounts.

Egypt is, in many ways, the classic hydrological culture, and water requirements underlie every facet of life. Therefore, it is hardly surprising that estimates for supply and demand vary wildly. The most optimistic observers estimate a very small surplus. These calculations depend principally on four factors:[9]

* Extent of agricultural expansion through desert reclamation program
* Crop water requirements per hectare in the Old and New Lands (including conveyance losses in the irrigation distribution system)
* Completion schedule of upper Nile water conservation projects
* Extent of drainage water reuse in Egypt

By 1990, the Egyptian Master Water Plan foresees a surplus of over 8,000 MCM per year. John Waterbury's assessment indicates a deficit of some 4,000 MCM annually. Therefore, to expand its cultivated area, Egypt has three options:

* To increase the efficiency of the irrigation system and improve farm water management practices
* To utilize more efficient irrigation and drainage technologies
* To increase the re-use of drainage water

Statistics for Sudan are even less reliable and more contradictory; deficits almost as high as 14,000 MCM per year have been forecast for the 1990s. These predictions, however, result directly from plans to make the Sudan a major world agricultural producer. These plans are overly optimistic given local drainage and soil conditions.

As it enters Egypt, the average annual discharge of the Nile is approximately 85,000 MCM; of this, 25,000 MCM is derived from the White Nile, with its headwaters in Sudan and Uganda, and the remaining 60,000 MCM comes from the Blue Nile (50,000 MCM) and the Atbara (10,000 MCM), both

15

rising in Ethiopia. The first extensive Nile Water Agreement was reached in 1929; particular constraints were put on the Sudan, as Egypt received 48,000 MCM and Sudan received a mere 4,000 MCM per year, leaving one-third of the discharge to pass unused to the Mediterranean. This agreement was not seriously challenged for some 20 years, owing to Egypt's political dominance and the Sudan's slow pace of economic development.

In the 1950s tension increased between the two riparians, brought to a head by controversy over the Aswan High Dam project. Relations deteriorated further, to military confrontation in 1958. One result of this deterioration was that Sudan, disregarding the 1929 agreement, raised the height of the Sennar Dam. A new regime in Sudan, however, was more sympathetic and an Agreement for the Full Utilization of the Nile Waters was signed in 1959. The Aswan High Dam was completed by 1971, yielding some 32,000 MCM of available water, of which 10,000 MCM was lost annually through evaporation from the vast Lake Nasser. Of the remaining 22,000 MCM per year, Egypt received 7,500 MCM and Sudan 14,500 MCM; as of 1988, there has been no conflict over this allocation. Furthermore, there have been several joint projects undertaken since the mid-1970s, the largest being the Jonglei Canal scheme (at present halted by the Sudanese civil war) to cut a waterway through the Sudd marshes. If completed, this scheme would recover 4,700 MCM of water annually.[10]

Future developments, however, are far more complex and controversial. In particular, those involving the other African states will greatly affect the geopolitics of the basin. It is reasonable to assume that the long-term foreign policy interests of Egypt in Ethiopia, Uganda, and Zaire may be attributed in no small measure to the need to safeguard Egypt's crucial water supply. Since the advent of a Marxist regime in Ethiopia, that country has figured prominently in Egyptian thinking. In particular, there is anxiety about the possibility of politically motivated dam building. Given the current state of the Ethiopian economy, such an event seems unlikely.

The other riparian states are highly critical of possible Egyptian plans to supply Nile water to the Sinai and even to the Negev Desert of Israel, and of the possible Sudanese plan to provide 20 MCM per year by pipeline to Saudi Arabia. Given the deteriorating water situation in the basin, however, any scheme to pipe water from it seems unlikely to be implemented.

Other Key Basins

Although the Litani River lies entirely within the official boundaries of Lebanon, its lower course is close to the headwaters of the Jordan and is in Israeli-controlled territory. The discharge averages 700 MCM per year and, with the high precipitation of the Lebanon mountains, fluctuates comparatively little. The Litani River project was initiated by the government to provide both irrigated area and electricity. The essential features of the program were completed by 1966 and resulted in the flooding of Lake Qirwan and a redistribution of waters in the Bekaa Valley. The scheme included the diversion of part of the flow to the Awali, and this further reduced seasonal variability within the main river.

The key event, however, was the 1982 invasion of southern Lebanon by Israel, which gained control of the lower Litani and the Qirwan reservoir. The Israeli intention to occupy a 45km-wide security zone was interpreted as an attempt to annex the Litani prior to developing a diversion scheme. This claim has been strongly denied by the Israelis, and there is little evidence of such intentions with regard to the Litani, although the possibility has been discussed. The major objection would seem to be that, with upstream abstraction, there is insufficient discharge in the lower Litani to justify the major engineering required. The fact remains, however, that the Litani represents the only additional surface supply of high-quality water within reach of Israel, and further disputes seem inevitable.

The Orontes also rises in Lebanon, but flows for only 35km before entering Syria. The mean discharge of the Orontes is put at approximately 800 MCM per year, but this fluctuates considerably with the seasons. There are no major water projects in Lebanon, and, indeed, discharge from the Orontes is ample for any requirements. In the middle section of its course, the Syrian government implemented the Ghab Project, the main part of which was completed in 1967. This resulted in the irrigation of some 70,000 hectares.

Only the short, lowest section of the Orontes flows through Turkey and has attracted comparatively little development. Thus, the basin would appear to offer little in the way of potential for water geopolitics. On the other hand, as Turkey's requirements grow, and given other possible disputes between Turkey and Syria over water, there is always the possibility of confrontation at some time in the future. At the other end of the valley, Syria has expressed a fear of possible Israeli occupation. At present, however, the Orontes basin is a model of cooperation, a very unusual situation in the Middle East. Possible disturbances are purely conjectural.

OTHER ASPECTS OF WATER GEOPOLITICS

Competition for subsurface water is more covert. Nonetheless, as the boundaries of both shallow and deep aquifers do not coincide with political frontiers, there is obvious potential for conflict. A classic case of transborder subsurface abstraction occurs in northwestern Oman. Ideal natural recharge conditions exist to the east of Buraimi, and over time these have produced particularly high-yielding aquifers. In the 1980s, overpumping in Al Ayn (United Arab Emirates) has resulted in a dramatic decline in the water table beneath Buraimi. Within that period, a fall of at least 50m has been recorded. There are many similar geological configurations throughout the Middle East, providing an obvious potential for the recurrence of this problem. Geopolitical difficulties may even result from the large-scale use of water from deep aquifers. For example, the immense pumping program in Libya must affect potential for development in the adjacent regions of Egypt.[11]

CONCLUSIONS

Because there is very low rainfall and, therefore, low recharge rates throughout the Middle East, there is a great shortage of naturally occurring fresh water. There are deep "fossil water" aquifers, but depletion of these is a contentious hydrological issue. In the case of both surface and groundwater supplies, potential and actual geopolitical disputes result from the noncoincidence of political and resource boundaries. Indeed, it may be predicted with confidence that in the future water will increasingly become a key factor in confrontations over political frontiers. As Mark Twain once said, "Whiskey is for drinking, water is for fighting."

NOTES

1. G. O. Barney, The Global 2000 Report to the President. The Technical Report, Volume Two, The Council on Environmental Quality and the Department of State, 1980, pp. 137-159.
2. J. Bodgener, "Oman Develops Skills Ancient and Modern," The Middle East Economic Digest, 10 August 1984, p. 38.
3. T. Odone, "Manmade River Brings Water to The People," Middle East Economic Digest, 10 August 1984, pp. 39-40.
4. M. Keen, "Cheaper, Purer Water from the Sun," Water and Sewage, 5 August 1985, pp. S14-S16.
5. Thomas Naff and R. C. Matson, Water in the Middle East: Conflict or Cooperation (Boulder, Colo: Westview Press, 1984), p. 236.
6. Ibid.
7. J. A. Allan, "Irrigated Agriculture in the Middle East: The Future," in Agriculture Development in the Middle East, Peter Beaumont and Keith McLachlan, eds. (New York: John Wiley and Sons, 1985), p. 150.

8. J. Perera, "Water Geopolitics," The Middle East, February 1981, pp. 47-54.

9. D. Whittington and K. E. Haynes, "Nile Water for Whom?" in Agricultural Development in the Middle East, Peter Beaumont and Keith McLachlan, eds. (New York: John Wiley and Sons, 1985), pp. 125-149.

10. Ann Charnock, "Nile Schemes Bring Benefits and Problems," Middle East Economic Digest, 10 August 1984, p. 38.

11. Odone, op. cit., note 3, supra.

TABLE 1.1
Surface and Ground Water Availability
(Units: '000 m^3 per capita per annum)

Country	Year 1971	2000	Population Increase (%)
Algeria	2.2	1.0	111
Arabian Peninsula states	0.7	0.3	106
Cyprus	0.06	0.05	22
Egypt	0.1	0.05	111
Iran	6.0	2.5	145
Iraq	3.6	1.3	173
Libya	3.7	1.2	198
Morocco	2.1	0.9	132
Sudan	4.0	1.9	107
Syria	3.0	1.0	165
Tunisia	0.9	0.4	126
Turkey	4.9	2.3	118

Source: G. O. Barney, The Global 2000 Report to
the President. The Technical Report, Volume Two,
The   Council   on   Environmental   Quality   and   the
Department of State, 1980, pp. 137-159.

2

The Legal Regime
of the Nile River Basin

Raj Krishna

INTRODUCTION

The Nile traverses 5,611 kilometers from its source in Lake Victoria and 4,500 km from its source in Lake Tana in Ethiopia to the Mediterranean. The Nile basin is estimated to contain an area of 3,030,700 km^2. Its breakdown among the nine basin states is shown in Table 2.1.

Lake Victoria is fed by the Kuja, Awach (or Kiboun), Miriu (or Sondu), Nyando, Nzoia, Sio, and Yala rivers of Kenya and the Mara and the Kagera rivers to the south in Tanzania. The Kagera River also drains the territories of Rwanda and Burundi and thus includes these countries within the Nile basin.

The Nile in Uganda provides the drainage outlet to Lake Victoria. The discharge passes through the Owen Falls Dam (1954) and flows through Ugandan territory to Lake Kyoga and then westward to Lake Mobutu Sese Seko formerly Lake Albert. From this lake the river traverses to the north as the Albert Nile. In the Sudds of southern Sudan the river is known as Bahr el Gebel, and beyond Makalal, as the White Nile. At Khartoum, it is joined by the Blue Nile, which drains Lake Tana in Ethiopia, and 174 kilometers further north of Khartoum it is joined by the Atbara River, also from Ethiopia. After this, the

---

This article reflects the views of the author and should not be interpreted as expressing the views of the World Bank.

23

Nile makes a southwesterly loop in the Sudan, flows in a northerly direction, and crosses into Egypt at Wadi Halfa, finally emptying into the Mediterranean.

Regarding the contribution of waters to the Nile by various riparians, varying estimates have been proposed. One Egyptian authority, Gamal Moursi Badr, suggests that 84 percent of the total annual discharge of the Nile is contributed by Ethiopia and only 16 percent by Uganda, Zaire, Kenya, Tanzania, Burundi, and Rwanda.[1] Garretson believes that between April and September, the Blue Nile supplies 90 percent and in the low season only 20 percent of the flow reaching Khartoum.[2] Yet another writer, C. O. Okidi, estimates that, of the water flowing north of Khartoum, between 75 and 80 percent is contributed by Ethiopia and between 20 and 25 percent by the Lake Plateau of Central Africa.[3] Waterbury is of the view that in the twelve-month water year Ethiopia contributes 86 percent and the Lake Plateau 14 percent, whereas during the flood period, Ethiopia's contribution rises to 95 percent.[4] The Sudan and Egypt contribute no water to the Nile.

The annual flow entering Egypt is estimated at 84 billion cubic meters (BCM). This 84 BCM was also used as the figure for the mean annual discharge for the 1959 Agreement between Egypt and the Sudan. And this figure, in turn, was based on the flow data for the period 1900–1959. Waterbury points out that this mean annual discharge turns out to be too modest when compared to the data for an entire century, 1880–1980. He indicates that the period 1900–1959 was marked with a series of low floods and that there is some evidence, although very weak, of a new rise in 1960. Thus, Waterbury maintains that the mean annual flow for the hundred years up to 1980 is 89.7 BCM or an average of 3 BCM more per annum than was contemplated in the Agreement of 1959.

It is commonly accepted that Egypt began irrigation from the Nile almost 6,000 years ago. For more than five millennia this irrigation took the form of flooding. It was only in the nineteenth century that perennial irrigations began to replace the irrigation by flooding.

Modern control works began in Egypt with the construction of the Damietta barrage and the Rosetta barrage which was completed in 1861. Because of a greater need for water in the low season, the Aswan Dam was completed in 1902 to provide 1 BCM of stored water. More intensive and investigative planning followed in Egypt. In 1920, Egypt completed a comprehensive review of its estimated needs and those of the Sudan and proposed five projects to meet such requirements. Because this report came under severe criticism in Egypt, a commission was appointed in 1920 consisting of one nominee of the government of India (as chairman), one nominee from Cambridge University, and a nominee from the U.S. government. No agreement could be reached on the basis of the report of this commission. In 1925 a new commission was named, made up of a representative of the Egyptian government, a representative of the British government, and a Dutch engineer. The recommendations of this commission led to the Nile Waters Agreement of 1929.

In 1935 Egypt and the Sudan reached an Agreement on a dam project at Lake Tana that was modified in 1946 to increase the capacity to 25-30 BCM. These Agreements did not make much headway, as Ethiopia made no proposals in this regard. Egypt, however, had better success with the Owen Falls in Uganda. Under an Agreement between the United Kingdom and Egypt, the dam at Owen Falls would ensure that the flow from Lake Victoria would not fall below 44 million cubic meters (MCM) a day.

After World War II, Egypt prepared various proposals for major development of the Nile waters. It was left to President Nasser to announce the Egyptian proposal to build the High Dam at Aswan. The dam was to be 5 km in length and 100 meters high. Two million feddans (840,000 hectares) were expected to be reclaimed in Egypt, and 700,000 feddans (294,000 hectares) were to be converted to perennial irrigation. Hydropower generation was expected to exceed 4 billion kilowatt (kw) hours. The Sudanese government objected to the project on various grounds. After long and difficult negotiations, Egypt and the

Sudan signed an Agreement in 1959 paving the way for the construction of the High Dam.

TREATY ARRANGEMENTS REGARDING THE NILE

The United Kingdom entered into several treaty arrangements with other powers regarding the Nile. It has been pointed out that these arrangements "had the common objective of securing recognition of the principle that no upper-basin State had the right to interfere with the flow of the river, in particular to the detriment of Egypt."[5] Among the stipulations of these arrangements are the following.

1. Italy and the United Kingdom signed a Protocol on 15 April 1891. Article III of the Protocol provided that "the Government of Italy undertake not to construct on the Atbara any irrigation or other works which might sensibly modify its flow in the Nile."

2. The other treaty that is relevant is the Ethiopia-United Kingdom Treaty Regarding the Frontiers between the Anglo-Egyptian Sudan, Ethiopia, and British Eritrea of 15 May 1902. Under Article III, the emperor of Ethiopia promised "not to construct or allow to be constructed any works across the Blue Nile, Lake Tsana or the Sobat, which would arrest the flow of their waters into the Nile except in agreement with His Britannic Majesty's Government and the Government of the Sudan."

3. The Treaty of 9 May 1906 between the United Kingdom and the Independent State of the Congo to "Redefine Their Respective Spheres of Influence in Eastern and Central Africa" provided that the government of the Independent State of the Congo undertake not to construct, or allow to be constructed, any work on or near Semliki or Isango rivers that would diminish the volume of water entering Lake Albert, except in agreement with the Sudanese government (Article III).

4. The concern for Egypt's interests was also reflected in the tripartite Agreement between Great Britain, France, and Italy of 13 April 1906 and in the London Declarations, as well as in the Exchange of Notes at Rome between Italy and the

United Kingdom of 1925.

5. The Nile Waters Agreement (1929), which was in the form of an exchange of notes between the United Kingdom and Egypt, constituted an important landmark in the history of the Nile River. One of the most significant clauses of the Agreement was:

> Save with the previous agreement of the Egyptian Government, no irrigation or power works or measures are to be constructed or taken on the River Nile and its branches, or on the lakes from which it flows, so far as all these are in the Sudan or in countries under British administration, which would, in such a manner as to entail any prejudice to the interests of Egypt, either reduce the quantity of water arriving in Egypt, or modify the date of its arrival, or lower its level.

The 1929 Agreement further stipulated that when such works are to be constructed they would be under the direct control of the Egyptian government. It was also agreed that before undertaking these works, Egypt should agree with the local authorities in the Sudan on measures safeguarding local interests. The contribution of the 1929 Agreement to the legal regime of the Nile is significant. First, it showed a recognition on the part of the parties concerned of the principle of established rights. Insistence on the recognition of its natural and historic rights has been the most fundamental element of the Egyptian policy approach to the Nile waters. Second, the principle of equitable sharing also gained recognition. Thus, the Agreement reserved all the Nile's natural flow during the low season--from 19 January to 15 July (at Sennar)--for Egypt's use. The Sudan, on the other hand, was given the right to appropriate waters by the Sennar Dam from surplus waters of the summer.

6. The Nile regime established by the Agreement of 1929, was supplemented three times: first, by the Jebel Awlia Compensation Agreement of 1932; later, by another Agreement concerning

the working arrangements for this dam; and finally, by an Egyptian Declaration of 1949. These supplements were followed by a reported Agreement in 1952 in respect to the Fourth Cataract Dam; the text of this Agreement is not available, but some authorities have referred to it.

7. Other Agreements that preceded the Sudano-Egyptian Agreement of 1959 are the Agreement between Italy and Great Britain of 1925 granting Great Britain the right to build a barrage at Lake Tana and the Agreement relating to Owen Falls Dam at Lake Victoria. It may be pointed out that although the Nile regime could be extended to Uganda, it failed to be extended to Ethiopia.

8. The 1959 Agreement between Egypt and the Sudan marked the culmination of attempts to set up a definitive regime of the Nile between these two states. Some features of this Agreement may now be noted.

* The title of the Agreement proclaimed it to be for the "full utilization of Nile waters," making it clear that the Agreement of 1929 "only regulated a partial use of the natural river."
* This Agreement did not repeal or abolish the Agreement of 1929.
* The Agreement recognized the established rights of the parties. The quantities of water actually used by Egypt up to the date of the Agreement constitute the established right of Egypt. This right was fixed at 48 BCM annually. The Sudan's established right, similarly computed, was fixed at 6 BCM per year.
* The Sudan agreed to the construction of the High Dam at Aswan, and Egypt permitted the Roseries Reservoir on the Blue Nile and any other works deemed necessary by the Sudan to exploit its share.
* The net increase resulting from the construction of the High Dam calculated after deducting the acquired rights of parties plus the loss caused by storage, estimated at 10 BCM, was distributed

28

between the two riparians. Of the 22 BCM estimated to be the net increase, Egypt was to receive 7.5 and Sudan 14.5. The total allocation thus amounted to 55.5 BCM for Egypt and 18.5 BCM for Sudan. Any increase in the net benefit, as a result of an increase in the mean annual flow of 84 BCM, was to be shared equally between the two States.

* The Sudan agreed to advance a water loan to Egypt from its share to enable Egypt to meet its agricultural expansion needs, provided that the loan would not exceed 1.5 BCM and its use would not extend beyond November 1977. It may be that the loan has extended well beyond 1977.

* The Agreement also made a provision of compensation of 15 million Egyptian pounds from Egypt to the Sudan.

* The Sudan agreed to undertake, in agreement with Egypt, projects for increasing Nile waters by preventing water wastes in the marshes of Bahr el-Gebel, Bahr el-Zaref, Bahr el-Ghazal and its tributaries, the Sobat River and its branches, and the Nile basin. Provision was also made for Egypt to carry out projects aimed at increasing Nile waters at a time when the Sudan does not need any additional supply.

* A permanent Joint Technical Committee comprising equal numbers of representatives from both states was to be established.

* An interesting provision in the Agreement relates to the course of action specified for dealing with the other riparians and for the consequences that may result from the claim of other riparians. It reads as follows:

1. In case any question connected with Nile waters needs negotiations with the governments of any riparian territories outside the Republic of Sudan and the United Arab Republic, the two Republics shall agree beforehand on a unified view in accordance with the investigations of

29

the problem by the Committee. This
unified view shall then form the basis of
instructions to be followed by the
Committee in the negotiations with the
governments concerned.

Should such negotiations result in an
agreement to construct works on the Nile
in territories outside the two Republics,
the Permanent Joint Committee shall then
assume the responsibility to contact the
concerned authorities in those territories
in order to lay down all the technical
details in connection with the execution
as well as the Working Arrangements and
maintenance of the works in question.
After agreement on these points with the
governments concerned, the Committee shall
supervise the execution of the technical
provisions of such agreements.

2. Since other riparian countries on
the Nile besides the Republic of Sudan and
the United Arab Republic claim a share in
the Nile waters, both Republics agree to
study together these claims and adopt a
unified view thereon. If such studies
result in the possibility of allotting an
amount of the Nile water to one or the
other of these territories, then the value
of this amount as at Aswan shall be
deducted in equal shares from the share of
each of the two Republics.

The Permanent Joint Technical
Committee shall make arrangements with the
concerned authorities in other territories
in connection with the control and
checking of the agreed amounts of Nile
water consumption.

AGREEMENT FOR HYDROMETEOROLOGICAL SURVEY OF LAKES
VICTORIA, KYOGA, AND ALBERT

In 1950, Egypt and Britain had already agreed
to cooperate in a meteorological and hydrological
survey of Lake Victoria (Exchange of Notes of
1950). There were some contacts between the
Sudan-Egypt Joint Technical Committee of the Nile

30

and an East African Nile Waters Coordinating Committee, made up of representatives of Kenya, Uganda, and the erstwhile Tanganyika. The idea was to discuss the discharges at Owen Falls Dam, future storage of waters in Lake Victoria and Lake Albert, and the requirements of East African countries for irrigation in the lake drainage area. In 1961, the three East African countries requested the UN Expanded Programme of Technical Assistance to assist in a hydrometeorological survey of the Victoria Lake catchment. A report was submitted to the three governments in 1963. As the three states were convinced that the Lake Kyoga and Lake Albert catchment areas should also be included in a further study, they invited Egypt and the Sudan. As a result, the representatives of the five states prepared a proposal in 1965 for a hydromet survey of the three lakes and signed a Plan of Operation in August 1967 with the United Nations Development Program (UNDP). The World Meteorological Organization was to be the executing agency. Later consultations were held with Rwanda and Burundi to extend the project area to cover the drainage area of Lake Victoria in these two states.

Another notable development was the Agreement for the Establishment of the Organization for Management and Development of the Kagera River Basin. This agreement was signed by Burundi, Rwanda, and Tanzania in 1977. The powers of the organization are very extensive. It is a vehicle for river development as well as a regulatory body. Uganda joined the organization in May 1981.[6]

CONCLUSIONS

As this brief survey has shown, there is no agreement that binds all the riparian states. Moreover, the population increases in Sudan and Egypt and the consequent increase in the demand for water are likely to require a revision of the water allocation made in 1959. The Jonglei Canal project in Sudan, which is aimed at decreasing the loss of Nile water in the Sudd, has increasingly come under attack from environmentalists. The critics argue that this will change the weather and rain patterns in southern Sudan and will cause flooding of the Sobat Valley in Ethiopia. To avoid flooding, the discharge at Owen Falls will have to be further controlled by Uganda. This in turn may result in damage, as it is authoritatively maintained that between 1961 and 1964, Lake Victoria's level rose a surprising 2.5 meters.

In 1976, newspapers carried reports of Egyptian plans to reclaim nearly 324,000 hectares of desert land in the Suez Canal area and the Sinai. Egypt has already started supplying waters through pipelines under the Suez to the Sinai for desert irrigation. One report estimated that 1.5 MCM of Nile water will be transferred to the Sinai to cultivate 12,150 hectares. In 1981, President Sadat reputedly offered to Prime Minister Begin to provide Jerusalem with 1 MCM of Nile water daily in exchange for the solution of the Palestinian problem and the liberation of Jerusalem. Future plans for the use of Nile water in the East African States—Ethiopia, Rwanda, Burundi, and Zaire—are still not known with any degree of certainty. Regarding the countries around Lake Victoria, particularly Kenya and Tanzania, Okidi has hinted at the possibility that these countries "might have a unique cluster of interests in the Lake that could be poised against those of the lower riparians, especially the Sudan and Egypt, in any attempt to work out an up-to-date legal regime for the Victoria and Nile waters."[7]

No discussion of future problems and prospects relating to the Nile can be complete without reference to Ethiopia, which Waterbury terms the "great unknown." Ethiopia's neighbors receive about 100 BCM of water annually from Ethiopia. "Not only does Ethiopia export water but, as well, the rich soils that have made the fortune of Sudanese and Egyptian agriculture. The price has been the profound and irremediable erosion of the Ethiopian highlands. It has been estimated that something like 2,000 tons of solid materials per km^2 are washed away annually in the highlands....These soils, over the millennia, have been deposited on the broad, flat plain between the White and Blue Niles upstream of Khartoum and in the Delta in Egypt. More recently billions of M^3 of silt have been deposited in the reservoirs at Roseries, Sennar, Khashm al-Girba, and at Aswan."[8]

Ethiopia undoubtedly enjoys a preeminent position on the Nile, and its attitude is of crucial importance for the future. As noted previously, the Italian-British Agreement of 1925 gave Great Britain the right to construct a dam at Lake Tana. This Agreement was rejected and a protest lodged by Ethiopia with the League of Nations in 1925. Sayed Hosni points out that all parties finally agreed that the Agreement was not binding on Ethiopia, and the question was dropped.[9] Ethiopia, for its part, went ahead and awarded a concession to a U.S. firm to build the dam. The British government reacted strongly to the Ethiopian plan. J. G. White Engineering Corporation of New York carried out the engineering studies between 1930 and 1934. In May 1935, Ethiopia formally proposed the plan to Egypt, the Sudan, and the United Kingdom, but the British turned it down. Later, a survey of the Blue Nile carried out by the U.S. Bureau of Reclamation between 1958 and 1963 produced seventeen volumes of findings. In 1977 Ethiopia announced that over the short term as many as 92,000 hectares in the Blue Nile basin and 28,400 in the Baro would be brought under irrigation. Over the medium term, the total water abstraction might reach 4 BCM per year. Other proposed uses could also reduce the water of the Blue Nile at the Sudanese border by 5.4 BCM. Waterbury points out that, even "in the early 1960s that would have meant a major reduction in the supply available to Egypt and the Sudan. Today such a reduction would be near catastrophic."[10] In the early 1980s, there have been some sharp exchanges between Ethiopia and Egypt. Ethiopia is said to have charged that Egypt was misusing its share of Nile waters by diverting part of it to the Sinai for future use by Israel. Both the Egyptian army chief and President Sadat warned Ethiopia about taking actions against Egypt. President Sadat said, "We do not need permission from Ethiopia or the Soviet Union to divert our Nile water....If Ethiopia takes any action to block our right to the Nile waters, there will be no alternative for us but to use force. Tampering with the rights of a nation to water is tampering with its life and a decision to go to war on this score is indisputable in the international community."[11]

The Egyptian Master Water Plan--a joint effort of Egypt, the UNDP, and the World Bank-- estimates demand to reach 63.1 BCM by the year 2,000 on the basis of land reclamation at an average rate of 42,000 hectares per year from 1980-2000. On the other hand, Waterbury projects Egyptian demand to be 73 BCM by 1990, with a total supply availability of 68.9 BCM, thus leaving a shortage of 4.1 BCM. All these projections are based on several factors including: the Jonglei I and II[12]; the future uses in the Sudan; the rate of urbanization affecting old lands in Egypt and reclamation of new lands; and the water uses in Ethiopia. In 1983, Vujica Yevjevich recommended supplementing a small number of hard-core projects by a very large number of soft-core projects on the Nile. According to Yevjevich, "Sudan and Egypt, without counting the other upstream countries in the Nile River basin, have more potential, high-quality good lands for irrigation than there is water available for them in the river."[13]

Another discouraging aspect is that there is no single agreement relating to the Nile encompassing all the basin States. Existing agreements or arrangements, other than the 1959 agreement between the Sudan and Egypt, have been challenged. Godana, who has examined this aspect in some detail, has concluded as follows:

> The Sudan has recognised the "historic rights" of Egypt which, in the 1959 Agreement, have been fixed at 48 milliards of cu.m...[T]he views of the upper-basin States appear to be different. Ethiopia simply does not acknowledge any existing treaty or other obligations preventing it from freely disposing of the Nile waters on its territory. Undoubtedly, there does not seem to be any such obligation on Rwanda and Burundi outside custom. Kenya, Uganda and Tanzania...all reject the theory of the

perpetual duty, imposed on them by the 1929 Agreement, not to interfere with the flow of the waters of the Nile to the detriment of Egypt without the latter's consent, but they have accepted, as a temporary measure, pending the conclusion of a more equitable and comprehensive agreement for the division of the waters, to observe that duty. It would appear that the position of Zaire is similar. All in all, the upper-basin States do not share the view of the lower-basin States on the perpetual nature of the present regime.[14]

One can also discern a trend among African publicists, who regard the present legal regimes as the vestiges of "colonial-era" agreements, that "totally disregards the interests of the upper-basin States" and, therefore, consider them "untenable."[15] These views may not be shared by all authorities. Besides, international law imposes certain obligations on upstream and downstream riparians alike.

The picture, perhaps, is not as bleak as it is often painted. In general, African states have exhibited a lot more cooperation and a lot more vision in dealing with their international rivers than is true in many circumstances in many other parts of the world. Representatives of Nile basin countries (with the exception of Ethiopia) have been involved in the hydromet study referred to earlier. The representatives of the Nilotic countries met for a UNDP Workshop for Nile Basin Countries in Bangkok in January 1986. The workshop, with the exception of Ethiopia, approved the following recommendations:

1. It is essential that the riparian countries cooperate in sharing water resources for the benefit of all on an equitable and mutually beneficial basis for the effective development of the Nile basin.
2. The approach to be adopted for the comprehensive development of the water resources of the basin should be effective and should be suited to the specific needs of the Nile riparian countries.

3. Action in order to promote and to establish effective regional cooperation among the Nile riparian countries should be undertaken at the earliest possible opportunity.

4. The representatives of the Nile riparian countries invited UNDP to extend the necessary assistance to study, propose and establish appropriate machinery for effective cooperation among the Nile countries for harnessing the water resources of the Nile.

5. The representatives of the Nile riparian countries also invited UNDP to play a catalytic role required for mobilizing and organizing the assistance from the bilateral and international donor community, in support of the Nile development effort.

6. The representatives of the Nile riparian countries requested UNDP to extend its assistance to the data collection programme in the Nile basin to Ethiopia.

7. The Nile riparian countries should meet periodically at the appropriate ministerial level to consult one another to strengthen the existing cooperation among riparian states and to ensure effective planning and implementation of the Nile basin development programme.

To that effect, the workshop requested UNDP to organize, as soon as possible, a meeting among the Nile riparian countries in order to examine concrete proposals for the setting up of a coordinating technical machinery to assist the riparian countries in the planning and implementation of the Nile basin development program.

It should be noted that recently a proposal was made to establish a Nile Basin Commission comprising all the nine riparian countries.[16] In the proposal the Nile river basin is regarded as "a hydrological unit"; the wording refers to the "best utilization of the waters of the Nile Basin without prejudice to the severing [sic] rights of the respective member states." This phrase would appear to include Egypt's historic rights. The Nile Basin Commission is vested with regulatory functions as well as with a limited developmental role. Thus, it is authorized to undertake "drought and flood control measures in the Nile basin." The commission is envisaged to have an executive secretariat. Although only a proposal, the conception is, nevertheless, a luminous milestone on a long and tortuous road.

Unlike some rivers that have been known as "rivers of sorrow," because of the floods, the changes in their course, and the havoc they have wrought, the Nile has been called, by Sir William Willcocks, the "most gentlemanly" of all the rivers of the world.[17] There is no reason to think that the Nile states will resolve the problem in any fashion not in keeping with the temperament of the river.

NOTES

1. G. M. Badr, "The Nile Waters Question: Background and Recent Development," #15 Egyptian Review of International Law, (1959) pp. 94-95. For other Egyptian estimates, see Albert H. Garretson, "The Nile River System," Proceedings of the American Society of International Law at its Fifty-Fourth Annual Meeting held at Washington, D.C., April 28-30, 1960, (1960) p. 136.

2. Albert H. Garretson, "The Nile Basin," in A. H. Garretson and R.D. Hayton, The Law of International Drainage Basins (New York: Oceana Publications, Inc., 1967) pp. 256-259.

3. C. O. Okidi, "Legal and Policy Regime of Lake Victoria and Nile Basins," #20 Indian Journal of International Law, (1980), pp. 395-399.

4. John Waterbury, Hydropolitics of the Nile Valley (Syracuse University Press, 1979) p. 23.

5. B. A. Godana, Africa's Shared Water Resources: Legal and Institutional Aspects of the Nile, Negev and Senegal River Systems, (London: Frances Pinter, 1985) p. 197.

6. Accession de l'Ouganda a l'Accord portant création de l'organization pour l'aménagement et le développement du bassin de la rivière Kagera. Bujumbura, Le 19 Mai 1981. United Nations, Natural Resources Water Series No. 13, Treaties Concerning the Utilization of International Water Courses for

Other Purposes than Navigation, Africa, (New York, 1984) p. 70.

7. C. O. Okidi, op. cit., note 3, supra at p. 401.

8. John Waterbury, "Riverains and Lacustrines: Toward International Cooperation in the Nile Basin," Discussion Paper No. 107, (September 1982) p. 84.

9. Sayed Hosni, "The Nile Regime," Egyptian Review of International Law, #17, p. 70 and pp. 89-90.

10. Waterbury, op. cit., note 8, supra., p. 90.

11. "Egypt: Threat to Nile Water," African Recorder, Vol. 19, No. 14, (14 July 1980) pp. 5 and 396.

12. Jonglei I and II projects aimed at preventing the loss of water from the Nile in the swamps of Southern Sudan. Jonglei I included the excavation of a canal to capture the flood water at its off-take at Jonglei and to deliver the water to the White Nile. See Garretson, op. cit., note 2, supra., pp. 272-273. Jonglei I had a delayed start and several vicissitudes. See Waterbury, op. cit., note 4, supra., pp. 76-77 and 215. Because of the political situation in the South, the work on the canal has been suspended. The benefit to Egypt and the Sudan from Jonglei I is estimated at 4.81 BCM each. See Waterbury, op. cit., note 8, p. 36. From Jonglei II, which is the second stage of Jonglei I, each of the two riparians is estimated to receive an additional 2.4 BCM of water. Ibid. Jonglei II was originally expected to be completed by 1995.

13. Vujica Yevjevich, "The Nile River Basin: Hardcore and softcore water projects." Water International #8 (1983) pp. 23 and 33.

14. Godana, op. cit., note 5, supra., p. 197.

15. Ibid., p. 199.

16. The draft proposal for the Nile Basin Commission was made available to the author by Mr. Bakheit Makki of the Permanent Joint Technical Committee for Nile Waters in 1986. The draft proposal appears to differ from the proposal of 1972 referred to by Waterbury. See Waterbury, op. cit., note 8, supra., pp. 129 et seq.

17. A. I. Baddour, Sudanese-Egyptian

Relations: A Chronological and Analytical Study,
(The Hague: M. Nijhoff, 1960) p. 201.

TABLE 2.1
Nile Basin Breakdown

Country	km²	% of basin
Sudan	1,900,000	62.7
Ethiopia	368,000	12.1
Egypt	300,000	9.9
Uganda	232,000	7.7
Tanzania	116,000	3.8
Kenya	55,000	1.8
Zaire	23,000	0.8
Rwanda	21,500	0.7
Burundi	14,500	0.5

Source: Register of International Rivers, prepared by the Center for Natural Resources, Energy and Transport of the Department of Economic and Social Affairs of the United Nations (Pergamon Press, 1978) p. 5.

3

Jordan River Basin Water:
A Challenge in the 1990s

Selig A. Taubenblatt

During the 1990s, a number of countries in the Middle East will face major water shortages. Even those countries in which water is not in short supply will experience many problems related to water supply and waste-water disposal. Sound water resource development and management will be a constant challenge for the entire region.

In the Jordan River basin, the scarcity of water has weighed upon the region's day-to-day life since prehistoric times. Because of these water shortages, equitable apportionment among the riparian countries in the basin has always been difficult. In recent years, optimal water resource development of surface flows--though technically feasible--has not occurred, primarily because of the politics of the greater Middle East conflict.

Water is a key ingredient for the agricultural and industrial development of the basin. Adequate supplies of drinking water are essential for supporting the growing urban populations. As populations in Jordan, Israel, and the West Bank continue to grow, the water supply is expected to be inadequate. As demand grows and supply remains limited, water could have far-reaching political significance as a cause of conflict. With time, cooperation over development of vital resources will become even more important.

My purpose in this chapter is to provide an historical overview of the Jordan River basin and some of the water resource problems and solutions

41

that have been proposed, including the Johnston Plan. I also identify some of the key water problems and issues that should be addressed in the future. In order to be able to effectively deal with future solutions, we have to understand the historical evolution of the water dynamics of the basin and the political dynamics that have influenced the course of events.

THE JORDAN RIVER BASIN SYSTEM

Geopolitics in the Jordan River basin are linked very closely to the physical and geographic characteristics of the area. The Jordan River system begins in three headwater rivers: the Hasbani, which begins in Syria with a small part of its watershed in Lebanon; the Dan, which is entirely in Israel; and the Baniyas, which flows into Israel from springs in the north near Syria. These three rivers combine into the Jordan River in Israel, which then flows south into the Sea of Galilee (or Lake Tiberias). At the point where the Jordan River empties into the Sea of Galilee, there is a small piece of Israeli territory on the eastern side of the river, bounded on the south by the Yarmuk River, which flows into the Jordan from the east. This land area is known as the Adasiye, or Yarmuk, Triangle.

The Yarmuk and Jordan rivers converge south of the Sea of Galilee and then twist a tortuous course through the Jordan Valley, finally flowing into the salty depths of the Dead Sea some 113 kilometers away.

The Yarmuk River forms the boundary between Jordan and Syria and, in its lower reaches, between Jordan and Israel. South of the junction of the Jordan and Yarmuk rivers, the Jordan River is the boundary between Israel and Jordan. Thus, each of these tributaries is itself an international river.

In the Jordan Valley between the Sea of Galilee and the Dead Sea, the river flows into a deep gorge called the Zor, from which steep hills rise to the terraces of the Ghor. The West Ghor merges with the rolling hills that border the coastal plains while on the East Bank the Ghor

42

gives way to a vast plateau. From north to south in the Jordan Valley, rainfall diminishes rapidly and the climate becomes subtropical. Rain falls only from October to May, with the heaviest rains during the winter months. In the winter, the side streams feeding the Jordan River become rushing torrents that erode the land. In the summer, many of the streams are completely dry. Thus, the challenge for the riparian states, particularly Jordan and Israel, is to collect and store water during the winter months and make it available during the dry summer months, when water is in short supply. It should be emphasized that the waters of the Yarmuk and Jordan rivers, which are not diverted for use or stored, become more saline as they flow downstream, eventually flowing into the Dead Sea.

Among the major obstacles to the peaceful and efficient utilization of the Jordan River basin waters is their division among the four riparians--Israel, Jordan, Syria, and Lebanon. In the case of the Yarmuk River, Syria is an upper riparian to Jordan, and Jordan is an upper riparian to Israel. In the case of the Jordan River, Syria and Lebanon are upper riparians to Israel, and Israel is an upper riparian to Jordan.

PAST RIVER BASIN DEVELOPMENT PLANS

Since the 1930s, there have been numerous river basin development plans, which have been elaborated for the more effective utilization of the Jordan River basin system. A number of the recent proposals have taken into account earlier plans. Present and future solutions can best be understood in the context of the historic evolution of planning and development of the water resources of the Jordan River basin.

Past plans include: the Ionides Survey (1939), Lowdermilk Plan (1944), Hays Plan (1948), MacDonald Report (1951), All Israel Plan (1951), Bunger Plan (1952), Israeli Seven-Year Plan (1953), Main Plan/Unified Plan (1953), Cotton Plan (1954), Arab Plan (1954), Baker-Harza Plan (1955), Johnston Plan (1955), Israeli Ten-Year Plan (1956), National Water Plan (1956), East Ghor

Canal Stage I (1961-1980), Arab Headwater Diversion (1964), Maqarin Dam Plan (1975-1981), Jordan Valley Irrigation Stage II (1982-present).

All these plans, though prepared by different parties--Jordanian, Arab League, Israeli, and others--were attempts to develop the water resources of the Jordan River basin and to provide for effective use of this water. These plans recommended solutions for water resource development, water utilization, and storage.

THE JOHNSTON PLAN

The first effort at a unified joint development of the entire Jordan River basin system was presented to Israel and the Arab states in 1953 by special ambassador Eric Johnston, an envoy of President Dwight Eisenhower. This plan, later known as the Johnston Plan or the Jordan Valley Plan, developed during a series of negotiations by Ambassador Johnston with Israel and, separately, with the Arab states, over a twenty-four-month period from October 1953 to October 1955. This plan provided for the development of the surface water resources in the Jordan Valley basin, taking into account the interests of Israel and its Arab neighbors and aiming at an "equitable distribution" of water. Although most of the technical elements of the plan were eventually agreed upon by all the parties, formal agreements were never concluded, ostensibly because the Arab League decided on political grounds against formalizing the arrangements.

The principal elements of the Johnston Plan were:
1. <u>Storage</u>
   * A dam on the Yarmouk River near Maqarin, 126 meters high with a storage capacity of 300 million cubic meters (MCM), for irrigation and power generation of some 150 million kilowatt hours of electric power per year.
   * Storage of Yarmuk River flood flows in the Sea of Galilee, estimated at

44

eighty per year and requiring storage space for 300 MCM. Such actual storage was to be delayed for five years, pending review by an engineering board of the necessity of using the Sea of Galilee for storage of Yarmuk River water.

2. Distribution
    *   A diversion dam on the Yarmuk near Adasiye to facilitate diversion into the East Ghor Canal and, if necessary, to divert excess flood waters into the Sea of Galilee for later delivery to Jordan.
    *   A feeder canal from the Sea of Galilee to the East Ghor Canal.
    *   A siphon or other structure across the Jordan for conveying water from the East Ghor to the West.

3. Division of Waters
    *   The principle adopted for the division of waters was to assure that the Arab states would receive enough water to meet the needs of all their lands that can be feasibly irrigated. The allocations proposed were derived as follows:
        To Jordan: The residual water from the Yarmuk River (estimated at 377 MCM after allocation of 25 MCM to Israel and 90 MCM to Syria); 243 MCM from wadis and wells, and 100 MCM from the Jordan River/Sea of Galilee;
        To Syria: 90 MCM from the upper Yarmuk, 20 MCM from the Baniyas, and 22 MCM from the upper Jordan;
        To Lebanon: 35 MCM from the Hasbani;
        To Israel: The residual water from the Jordan River and 25 MCM from the Yarmuk River for the Adasiye Triangle. The total quantity of Jordan River water allocated to Israel was not specified in the formal documents but was computed as 361 MCM, after allocations to Syria and Jordan.

45

Thus, Jordan was to receive all the remaining water from the Yarmuk River after specific allocations for Syria and Israel, and Israel was to receive all the waters of the Jordan River after specific allocations to Syria and Jordan. The Johnston Plan included the West Bank in Jordan's water allocation. The Johnston Plan also provided for an impartial engineering board and a watermaster to supervise the operation of the water system in conformity with the plan.

It is clear that the Johnston negotiations did not result in agreements binding the parties under international law. Even at the technical level, there remained three unresolved issues: the quantity of water for the Adasiye Triangle; the role of the watermaster; and the amount of saline water to be included in the 100 MCM for Jordan from the Sea of Galilee. It is believed, however, that if it were not for political disputes, the remaining technical issues could have been resolved without difficulty.

Since the Johnston negotiations came to a halt in 1955, Israel and the Arab states have followed many of the principles enunciated in the plan, which has played a constructive role in providing a basis for "equitable water sharing" during the years that followed. The Johnston Plan, however, dealt with water resources development in the basin and historic water uses in the context of the 1950s; many changes have taken place since then in water availability and uses in both Israel and Jordan. It should also be noted that the Johnston Plan dealt only with the apportionment of surface water and did not address the distribution of groundwater.

Between the mid-1950s and the mid-1970s, Israel and Jordan continued to develop their water resources. Israel built the National Water Carrier, which pumps water from the northern part of the Sea of Galilee via a pipeline and canal to Tel Aviv and into the Negev for irrigation and agricultural development.

Jordan developed the East Ghor Main Canal in the Jordan Valley for irrigation, using Yarmuk River water. It also built the King Talal Dam on the Zarqa River to store water for irrigation use. As the population grew and demand for water increased, other tributaries and water sources in Jordan were also developed for irrigation and municipal consumption.

THE MAQARIN DAM PLAN

In 1974, the government of Jordan revived planning for the Maqarin Dam and in January 1975 approached the United States Agency for International Development (USAID) for assistance in financing the cost of a $1-million feasibility study. Subsequently, USAID loaned Jordan $5 million to assist with the engineering design for the dam and irrigation works and an additional $9 million for subsequent engineering design work, a total of $15 million.

The Maqarin Dam project, designated by the Jordanians as "Jordan Valley Irrigation Project Stage II," initially consisted of two principal elements: the Maqarin Dam and related structures; and irrigation works in the Jordan Valley. The initial objective of the project was to increase the availability of water for irrigation in the Jordan Valley. The government subsequently reallocated water that was to have been used for irrigation to municipal and industrial use (from 20 MCM to 120 MCM reallocated for municipal and industrial use annually), in recognition of the growth in demand for water in the northern plateau of Jordan.

In the feasibility study submitted in January 1978, construction of the Maqarin Dam was proposed to be undertaken in two phases. First, the dam was to be built to a height corresponding to a reservoir elevation of 150 meters, including foundations on which the dam could be subsequently raised to a reservoir elevation of 192 meters. Raising the dam and constructing a second dam downstream, tentatively located at Wadi Khalid, were to be the second stage. The review at the donor's meeting in April 1978 concluded that the cost of implementing the two-stage approach was uneconomically high, and thus it was recommended that the construction of the Maqarin Dam be undertaken immediately to its ultimate height.

The total cost of the project in 1979 was estimated at about $1 billion. As eventually formulated, the Maqarin Dam project was to include:

* A 170-meter high dam with a total storage capacity of 486 million cubic meters
* A diversion weir at Adasiye
* Diversion of the Wadi Raqqad (in Syria) into the Maqarin reservoir
* Extension of the East Ghor Main Canal by 14.5 km
* Electric-generating facilities of 20 MW at the Maqarin Dam, and 2 MW at the King Talal Dam;
* Construction of new irrigation systems estimated to cover about 10,000 hectares
* Conversion of existing gravity irrigation in the Jordan Valley to sprinkler irrigation

The construction of the Maqarin Dam project raised a number of riparian issues. Because Israel is a downstream riparian to Jordan on the Yarmuk River, the availability of water for the Yarmuk Triangle and for the West Bank had to be addressed. Impounding Yarmuk water flows in the Maqarin reservoir would have an impact on the downstream availability of water. Thus, Jordan had to reach agreement with Israel on water allocations and structures. Jordan also had to reach agreement with Syria, as water that would be stored behind the dam originated in the upper reaches of the Yarmuk River in Syria and because one side of the dam would be built on Syrian territory. In addition, the Maqarin Dam project was to have provided for the diversion of water from the Wadi Raqqad (in Syria) into the Maqarin Dam reservoir, with an average inflow of 48 MCM per year.

The Maqarin Dam project received considerable support from bilateral and multilateral lenders. Such support was expressed in the donors' meeting in London in April 1978. The U.S. Congress in fiscal year 1979/80 also committed to support the project with $150 million over three years. The bilateral lenders required that financing be conditioned: Jordan and Israel and Jordan and Syria had to resolve their riparian problems before funds would be made available.

At first, attention was concentrated on issues between Jordan and Israel, and the U.S. government assisted both countries in dealing with these issues. All the issues were not resolved, but progress was made nevertheless. Problems involving Jordan and Syria, however, increased in importance during the latter part of the 1970s, and relations between those two countries deteriorated. Eventually, Jordan's inability to reach agreement with Syria became an immediate cause of the indefinite postponement of the Maqarin Dam project in late 1980.

WATER FOR THE 1990S: THE PROBLEM AHEAD

In Israel, Jordan, and the West Bank the demand for water continues to grow well in excess of availability. In 1985, the population of Israel was estimated at 4.1 million; by 1995 it is expected to grow to about 5 million. In Jordan, the population in 1985 was estimated at 2.7 million and is expected to grow by 1995 to close to 4 million. In the West Bank the population in 1985 was estimated at about 800,000; by 1995 it could reach 1 million.

Water resources--surface and groundwater--in these three areas totalled about 2.5 billion cubic meters (BCM) in 1987 and are expected to grow only modestly. It is estimated that Israel accounts for about three-fourths of this total. About three-fifths of Israel's water supply comes from groundwater and the remainder from surface water. In contrast, Jordan derives about three-fourths of its water resources from surface water and the remainder from groundwater. The West Bank derives over four-fifths of its water resources from groundwater, including an aquifer shared with Israel.

Israel has tried to meet its growing demand through water reuse, recharging of groundwater aquifers; more efficient conservation methods, such as sprinkler and drip irrigation; and reallocation of water from agriculture to municipal and industrial uses. Jordan has also tried to deal more effectively with its limited water supply by diverting some water from agriculture to municipal and industrial uses (for example, the pipeline from the East Ghor Main Canal to the northern plateau). Jordan is developing its groundwater resources through continued exploration and by drilling to lower depths. Such groundwater resources, however, appear to be limited. Jordan is also increasing the height of the King Talal Dam by about 15 meters to increase the winter storage capacity for water to be used during dry summer months. Jordan has replaced surface canals and has introduced sprinkler and drip irrigation in its agriculture.

Nevertheless, additional water resources will be necessary as the populations grow in Jordan and Israel and as industry is developed. The only remaining surface water flow in the basin that has not been controlled is the Yarmuk River, and opportunities still exist that could increase the availability of water for Jordan and the West Bank. Such solutions, however, will require dams or barrages on the Yarmuk River, and possibly on the Jordan River, to help store water during the winter months to be released during the summer months when water is in short supply. Such storage could also supply water for municipal and industrial uses year-round. In the early 1980s, Jordan considered the feasibility of a water pipeline project that could bring about 160 MCM of water from the Euphrates in Iraq to the northern plateau in Jordan. The long distance, difficult terrain, and high cost have raised questions on the economic feasibility and possibilities for financing the project. As of 1988, this project has not been implemented.

During the coming decade, the following water questions and problems may have to be addressed by the riparian states if solutions are to be found to the growing water shortages.

1. If the Maqarin Dam project could proceed today, would it still be economically viable, particularly in light of increases in water use in southern Syria? Is the diversion of the Wadi Raqqad into the Maqarin reservoir still possible in view of the Syrian water uses? Is the Maqarin Dam financeable?

2. As relations between Jordan and Syria do not permit the Maqarin Dam project to proceed at this time, what are other dam alternatives downstream on the Yarmuk River that will permit more efficient uses of Yarmuk waters for Jordan, Israel (Yarmuk Triangle), and the West Bank? Could Yarmuk River storage in the Sea of Galilee for use in Jordan and the West Bank be considered a viable option in the right political climate?

3. Are there any opportunities for small dams or barrages on the Jordan River between the East Bank and West Bank to increase availability of water for more efficient use on both sides of the Jordan? What are the legal and political ramifications?

4. With the new technology, what are the opportunities for increasing groundwater availability in Jordan, Israel, and the West Bank?

5. Could large-scale power/desalination plants to desalt seawater and increase water availabilities help deal with the water problems in 1990s? In view of the decline in the price of oil, what has happened to the economic feasibility of seawater desalination? What are the opportunities for desalination of brackish water?

6. In 1987 King Hussein discussed a development plan for the West Bank with international donors that will cost about $750 million to about $1.2 billion over five years. What are the opportunities in this plan for water resource development and for increasing the supply of water for agricultural and municipal purposes?

7. Should the West Bank autonomy negotiations resume in the future, water allocation and control of water are likely to be major issues. The short supply of water on the West Bank will be a key determinant of the number of Palestinian refugees that could return there. How will this problem be dealt with? Another key issue will be the large western slope groundwater aquifer that is shared by the West Bank Palestinians and Israel.

8. Can substantial availability of foreign assistance resources help solve some of the water problems in the Jordan River basin, particulary in Jordan, Israel, and the West Bank?

9. Can the creation of an international water authority help in dealing with the riparian issues in the Jordan River basin? Can such issues best be dealt with bilaterally? What role, if any, should the United States play?

What is clear is that the water problem is getting worse. Water shortages will continue, and the potential for conflict in the 1990s will become greater. Although technology will play a major role, and engineering can help address some of these water problems, in the final analysis political factors may be more important to their resolution. Only regional cooperation among the parties can help resolve many of the issues we have discussed. Whether the political leadership in Jordan and Israel will be able to resolve these problems successfully in the context of the greater Middle Eastern conflict still remains to be seen. The challenge is enormous.

4

Desalination Technology: An Overview

Leon Awerbuch

STATUS OF DESALINATION

Desalination is the separation of water from dissolved impurities. Part of the water is recovered in comparatively pure form in a product stream. The dissolved impurities are concentrated in a waste stream (brine), which is discharged from the system as plant "blowdown," or "reject."

It is now technically feasible to generate large volumes of water of suitable purity through the desalination of brackish water and seawater. Wastewater has large potential for reuse, pending resolution of health uncertainties relative to toxicology and pathology. In the past thirty years, over 11.48 million cubic meters per day (m^3pd) of desalination capacity has been installed and contracted throughout the world. Although there have been growing pains, plants of up to 1 million cubic meters per day in one location and comprising single trains of about 40,000 m^3pd have performed reliably, delivering water of high purity at a cost acceptable in their respective regions.

On a worldwide basis, there are over 5,700 desalting units with capacities larger than 100 m^3pd. By far the greatest number of plants were established in the Middle East, particularly on the Arabian Peninsula; over 60 percent of the total desalting capacity is located in this region. The four largest builders of desalination plants are: Saudi Arabia, accounting for 30.2 percent of the total capacity; Kuwait, with 11.5 percent; the United Arab Emirates, with 11 percent; and the United States, with 10.9 percent.

Desalting plants have been installed in 105 countries and have been set up by 170 manufacturers. Data reproduced from the IDA (International Desalination Association) Worldwide Desalting Plants Inventory, published in February 1987, shows that 64.5 percent of all desalting plants operate on the multistage flash (MSF) principle, with the reverse osmosis (RO) process now accounting for 23.4 percent. Few multi-effect and vapor compression plants have been built, although the processes are now used more frequently.

Most of the large-scale desalination projects use seawater--a practically limitless resource--as feed. Seawater is used in 72.9 percent of all cases, compared to 24.9 percent using brackish water. At present, the desalination of municipal and industrial wastewater is a comparatively minor but rapidly expanding activity in the United States and other industrially advanced countries.

With the large capacity and large number of plants committed to desalination technology, the security of many nations depends on the reliability and performance of these desalination plants. The future of the desalination market is based not only upon additional need for new plants but also on significant replacement of the existing desalination units. Future technology will depend largely on energy costs and improvements in both membrane and distillation technology. A hybrid system, which combines the best features of distillation and reverse osmosis, may also be developed.

TECHNICAL COMPARISON OF PROCESSES

A controlling factor in process evaluation is the raw water source. Raw water delivered to a desalination plant may be divided into the following broad categories:

* seawater, which generally has a constant composition of about 35,000 mg/l (miligrams per liter) of dissolved solids throughout the world;
* brackish water, which is generally defined

54

as having no more than 10,000 mg/l of
dissolved solids;
* wastewater, which is available from a
variety of sources and has a wide range of
both the types of dissolved impurities and
their concentrations.

These distinctions are essential, because the
source of water determines both the types and
concentrations of impurities to be removed and the
type of pretreatment required to protect the
desalination process. In some cases, certain
processes cannot be applied to particular raw
water sources.

Multistage Flash Distillation

Multistage flash desalination accounts for
the major portion of fresh water currently
produced and is used primarily for desalting
seawater. This process has been in large-scale
commercial use since the late 1960s. In this
process, the feed is pressurized and heated to the
maximum plant temperature. When the heated liquid
is discharged into a chamber maintained slightly
below the saturation vapor pressure of the water,
a fraction of its water content flashes into
steam. The flashed steam is stripped of suspended
brine droplets as it passes through a mist
eliminator and condenses on the exterior surface
of heat transfer tubing. The condensed liquid
drips into trays as hot product water.
The unflashed brine enters a second chamber,
or stage, where it flashes to steam at a lower
temperature, producing a further quantity of
product water. Simultaneously, the distillate
from the first stage passes to the distillate tray
in the second stage, giving up some of its heat
and thereby lowering its temperature. The
flashing-cooling process is repeated from stage to
stage until both the cooled brine and the cooled
distillate are finally discharged from the plant
as blowdown brine and product water, respectively.
It is common practice to recycle a fraction
of the blowdown water, combined with feedwater,
through the entire circuit in order to extract an

additional fraction of its water content. The recirculating stream, flowing through the interior of the tubes that condense the vapor in each stage, serves to remove the latent heat of condensation. In so doing, the circulating brine is preheated to almost the maximum operating temperature of the process, simultaneously recovering the energy of the condensing vapor. This portion of the MSF plant is called the "heat recovery" section. The preheated brine is finally brought up to maximum operating temperature in a brine heater (or prime heater) supplied with steam from an external source.

At the cool end of the plant, a separate set of tubes is installed in several of the stages in a "heat rejection" section to remove the waste heat. The coolant there is generally not recycled brine, but the feedwater (in this example, seawater), of which the greater portion is discharged to waste. A small fraction of this coolant becomes preheated makeup water.

In principle, MSF is the simplest of the desalination techniques. Once the interstage openings are adjusted, the plant can operate for long periods without any resetting of flows. One kilogram of prime steam can produce several kilograms of product water. High-energy efficiency can be attained by

* incorporating many stages and a large heat transfer surface in the design of a plant;
* increasing the maximum brine temperature (but at the risk of increased corrosion and scale deposition);
* using heat-exchange tube material of high thermal conductivity or of an enhanced surface contour;
* incorporating suitable techniques for the control of scale formation;
* using design, operation, and maintenance procedures to prevent the local accumulation of noncondensible gases.

Multi-Effect Distillation

Multi-effect distillation (MED) is the oldest large-scale evaporative process. The basic principle is straightforward. The feedwater flowing over a heat transfer surface in the first chamber (effect) is heated by prime steam, resulting in evaporation of a fraction of the water content of the feed. The feed then descends as a thin film on the inside of vertical tubes. The partially concentrated brine is delivered to a second chamber (effect), maintained at a slightly lower pressure than the first effect. Likewise, the vapor liberated from the first effect feed is sent to the second effect. There it condenses on the heat transfer tubes, giving up its latent heat to evaporate an additional fraction of water from the brine flowing on the opposite wall of the tube. The process of evaporation-plus-condensation is repeated from effect to effect, each at successively lower pressure and temperature. The combined condensed vapor constitutes the product water. Here again, one kilogram of prime steam produces several kilograms of product water.

As in the MSF process, multi-effect distillation plants can be made more energy-efficient by increasing the number of effects and the heat transfer area or by increasing the maximum operating temperature. On the other hand, when low-cost heat is available, it is preferable to sacrifice some of the energy efficiency by operating at a lower temperature because of the resultant decrease in the rate of corrosion and scale formation. The low corrosion and scaling tendencies of the low-temperature multi-effect (LTME) process not only improve reliability and decrease operating costs but permit the construction of the plant from low-cost materials.

Vapor Compression Distillation

Vapor compression (VC) is similar to multi-effect distillation. The chief difference is that the vapor produced by the evaporation of the brine in the tubes is not condensed in a separate condenser or in a succeeding effect. Instead, it is returned by a compressor to the shell side of the same evaporator from which it originated, where it condenses on the tubes, giving up its latent heat to evaporate an additional portion of the brine. The energy for evaporation is derived not from a prime steam source, as in the preceding two distillation processes, but from the vapor compressor. The vapor compressor, in addition, raises the temperature of the vapor by its compressive action, thereby furnishing the driving force for the transfer of heat from vapor to brine.

VC shares with other distillation processes the ability to yield a product water of comparatively high purity. It is an established process with a good performance record. Minimal skill is required on the part of the operators.

Reverse Osmosis

Reverse osmosis (RO) desalination, another process using hydraulic pressure as its energy source, operates at ambient temperatures (under 40° C) in contrast to distillation, which operates in the range of 50° C to 120° C. In RO, a fraction of the water content of seawater or brackish water is driven under pressure through a semipermeable membrane, generally of organic materials.

RO has the advantage of low-temperature operation, which minimizes scaling and corrosion. Product purity, however, is only fair. Membrane processes also experience a sharp increase in energy demand as the feedwater concentration rises. In addition, membrane processes are very sensitive to specific contaminants in the feed and, hence, require careful pretreatment.

Electrodialysis

Unlike the preceding processes, which separate water from dissolved matter (predominantly inorganic salts), electrodialysis

(ED) removes the solutes from water. ED is not yet commercially available for the desalination of seawater. From an energy standpoint, the power consumption increases with the salinity of the feed. A highly saline feed has the further disadvantage of increasing back-diffusion of salt from the reject stream, thereby limiting the purity of the product water. Also disadvantageous is that ED cannot remove from the feed any material that is not ionized; consequently, the removal of silica is zero.

DESALINATION ECONOMICS

The cost of producing desalted water is a meaningful figure in comparing alternative processes and water sources. Distillation by a single-purpose plant is generally uneconomical for desalting either brackish water or seawater. The use of low-temperature waste heat from thermal power plants, however, can make distillation processes economically attractive.

The minimum cost for desalting brackish groundwater is approximately $0.30 per cubic meter using either RO or ED. Seawater desalting can be achieved at costs of approximately $0.81 to $1.47 per cubic meter for a dual-purpose distillation plant or at costs of $1.13 to $1.74 per cubic meter for single-purpose plants. In addition,

* for a single-purpose desalination plant, distillation is considerably more costly than the membrane process (reverse osmosis and electrodialysis) for both brackish water and seawater desalination;
* for a dual-purpose desalination plant that receives heat rejected by the power plant condensers, the water costs from low-temperature distillation are lower than the water costs from membrane process for seawater desalination;
* the new generation of high efficiency vapor compression plants is competitive with membrane processes for the desalination of seawater.

All of these costs are highly sensitive to energy costs and other site-specific conditions and should be regarded as generic for the processes considered.

In general, the largest contributions to the cost of product water come from capital costs (interest, amortization, and taxes) and energy costs. Also, because desalination is energy-intensive, the cost of energy often equals or exceeds the capital cost. Estimates for investment costs for a plant with an installed capacity of 20,000 cubic meters per day are shown in Table 4.1. The estimates specify the costs per cubic meter or gpd (gallons per day) of installed capacity. Where a market exists for both power and water, the dual-purpose concept permits the production of water at a lower cost, as steam of low value can be bled from the turbine at a temperature adequate for the desalination plant.

Comparative product water cost estimates are shown in Table 4.2. These generalized estimates include the following major cost components:

* capital
* energy
* operation and maintenance
* chemicals and general supplies
* membrane replacement (reverse osmosis and electrodialysis only).

These estimates are based on fuel oil cost of $18 per barrel, electricity cost of $.06 kwh, interest rate of 10 percent, and a 20-year life.

CONCLUSION

Now more than ever, water desalination technology is ready to solve water problems in arid and semiarid regions of the world. Current desalination technologies are fully capable of providing reliable sources of high-quality water for municipal and industrial purposes. The economics of desalination favor countries in which energy sources are less expensive. However, energy costs are not a prohibitive factor, especially if an increased and reliable water supply facilitated development of industry and tourism, thus producing additional revenues.

In many countries, primarily in the Middle East, adequate water supply is a basic security issue. Desalination plants in that part of the world are the main source of necessary water supplies. Although we do not expect any drastic reduction in desalination costs, we do envision a considerably larger utilization of the desalination technology.

Table 4.1
Comparative Investment Unit Costs
for 20,000 M^3PD Desalting Plant

Type Plant	$/m^3$ Installed	$/GPD Installed
1. Seawater feed		
MSF (economy ratio = 12)	1,980	7.50
Vapor compression	1,240	4.70
RO (two-stage)	990	3.75
Multi-effect evaporation		
horizontal tube (82° C)	1,510	5.70
horizontal tube-low		
temperature	1,360	5.15
2. Brackish water feed		
Reverse osmosis	225	2.85
Electrodialysis		
Reversal 2,000 mg/l	385	1.45
Electrodialysis		
Reversal 3,500 mg/l	517	1.96

Source: Bechtel National, Inc.,
Internal Studies

Table 4.2
Comparative Product Water Costs
for 20,000 M^{3}PD Desalting Plant

	$/m^3
1. Seawater Feed	
Single-purpose plant	
MSF (economy ratio = 12)	1.74
Vapor compression	1.13
Reverse osmosis (two-stage)	1.29
Dual-purpose	
MSF (economy ratio = 12)	1.47
Multi-effect evaporation	
horizontal tube (82° C)	0.96
horizontal tube-low temperature	0.81
2. Brackish water feed	
Reverse osmosis	0.32
Electrodialysis	
Reversal 2,000 mg/l	0.30
Electrodialysis	
Reversal 3,500 mg/l	0.40

Source: Bechtel National, Inc.,
Internal Studies

5

Water Problems, Solar Solutions: Applications of Solar Thermal Energy to Water Technologies

Donald E. Osborn, Raymond Sierka, and Medhat Latif

WATER PROBLEMS AND SOLAR SOLUTIONS

Water and energy are inexorably linked. The hydrologic cycle that produces our fresh water and weather is driven by solar energy. Water is required for the production of energy. It is used in cooling towers, the processing of energy minerals, and to drive such power systems as hydroelectric turbine, steam generators, and solar heating systems. Energy is required for the production of water supplies. From drilling and pumping requirements to wastewater treatment, our use of water is energy intensive.

Energy supplies are an especially critical factor in water reclamation efforts. For example, about 40 percent of the cost of large-scale desalination projects is for energy. In Saudi Arabia, the Ministry of Agriculture, which oversees the desalination efforts, generates more electricity than the Ministry of Electricity and Industry.[1]

Nearly one third of the earth's land is covered by deserts. Most of the southwestern United States and the Middle East are arid or semiarid lands. The need for water in arid areas of the world is becoming an increasingly critical issue as world population increases. The Middle East is one of the areas that has water supply problems and solar energy in abundance. Many arid areas, such as the U.S. Southwest, are becoming population centers with vast overdraws of groundwater and an increasingly complex combination of water shortages, water contamination, and strained energy supplies. Water scarcity issues are not just the topics of international policy conferences but are of concern for our children as well. The July/August 1987 issue of <u>3-2-1 Contact</u>, a magazine of the Children's Television Workshop, focused on water in a featured article titled "Are We Running out of Water?"

Fortunately for our future needs, a good match between water needs, energy scarcity, and solar resources exists. With the shifting economics of conventional energy sources, recent advances in solar technologies, and the increasing concern for the supply, treatment, and protection of water resources in the areas of abundant sunshine, it is time to turn a fresh eye to the application of solar energy to these complex and varied water problems. In this chapter we attempt to provide a preliminary perspective on solar energy applied to water reclamation efforts in the modern context.

We attempt to suggest some niches in which solar may find early application. No conclusive answers are provided or are even possible, given our current state of knowledge. This chapter is intended to raise more questions than it answers and to confront the conventional wisdom of the 1970s with the advances of the 1980s and an eye on the 1990s and beyond. It is our intent to stimulate a new awareness and interest in the possibilities of at least some solar solutions to some water problems.

SOLAR STATE-OF-THE-ART

Water reclamation efforts are often energy intensive, requiring both electrical and thermal energy. Although many solar power technologies have been around for centuries, the last decade has seen tremendous advances in our ability to produce electricity and high quality thermal energy from solar energy. Equally impressive strides have been made in reducing the costs of doing so.

The two major approaches to producing electricity from sunlight are photovoltaics (PVs) and solar thermal conversion. The advance in the state-of-the-art for solar electric power production by both approaches has been impressive. The solar thermal technologies have the additional advantages of being able to provide high-grade thermal energy and high-flux levels of sunlight for a variety of processing applications.

Photovoltaics

The advance of photovoltaics has been the most heralded of solar technologies, especially as its march toward widespread cost-effectiveness has been impressive. Photovoltaics employ modular, semiconductor devices to directly convert sunlight to electrical energy. When light strikes the photovoltaic, or solar, cell, electrons are freed in the semiconductor material and an electric current is generated. Groups of individual cells are combined to form PV modules. Although most PV modules are flat plate arrays, concentrating systems are also being developed to substitute less-expensive reflector or lens area for the high-cost solar-cell materials. About half of the cost of today's photovoltaic systems is in the modules and the solar cells that make them up. The rest is in balance-of-system components and installation needed for a complete power system.

Cost reductions in electric power production by PVs since the mid-1970s have been dramatic. From over $15 per kilowatt-hour (kwh) in 1975, PV costs have dropped to about $.40 per kwh in 1986. This decrease in cost has been accompanied by an increasing use of PV, from 300 kilowatts (kw) of PV systems produced in 1975 to over 13 megawatts (MW) of PV production capacity annually in 1986 (Figure 5.1). PV system applications have been steadily expanding from remote-site applications and consumer electronics toward bulk power production. Today, PVs provide cost-efficient electric power in areas only a few miles from power lines and as incremental power plant additions.

The downward trends of PV power costs are expected to continue with new advances in PV materials, system efficiencies, concentrator development, and manufacturing advances. The U.S. Department of Energy's long-term goals for PVs in the late 1990s translate to a thirty-year levelized cost of 6.5 cents per kwh (in constant 1982 dollars). This represents a viable, cost-effective electric power technology for bulk power production.

Solar Thermal

Although the advances of photovoltaics have been widely publicized, the achievements of solar thermal technologies have been less heralded but are equally dramatic. Solar thermal systems can provide thermal energy from low-temperature/low-grade heat to high-temperature/high-grade heat. The medium- to high-grade solar thermal systems can be used to generate electric power. Solar thermal systems can also be used to provide solar energy in the form of concentrated fluxes of photons that can have unique applications.

Currently, there are four major approaches to solar thermal electric and high-grade thermal power production: power towers, linear troughs, point-focus dishes, and solar salt ponds. Each of these systems can supply electricity or high-grade heat to provide the energy needed for conventional water reclamation techniques or can be used to drive specific solar techniques for water reclamation.

Power towers, also called central receiver systems, utilize large fields of heliostats, or tracking mirrors, to focus the sunlight to a receiver atop a central tower (Figure 5.2). The concentrated sunlight heats a heat-transfer fluid to between 530° C to $1,500^{\circ}$ C. This heat is then used to drive a turbine-generator to produce electricity just as a generator does in a conventional power plant. Thermal storage can be added to permit electric power production when the sun is not shining. Central receiver systems are generally designed to produce power in the tens of megawatts range or higher. An experimental demonstration system, Solar One, has successfully completed five years of testing, evaluation, and power production. Designed in 1979, Solar One began operation in 1982. This 10-MW pilot plant consists of a 61-m central receiver tower and

1,818 heliostats, each about 44.6 m^2. Steam at a temperature of 515° C is produced in the receiver. Solar One has exceeded every production goal established for it. The system peaks at 12 MW and has a thermal storage system, permitting four hours of up to 7 MW production.[2] Central receiver systems can also provide a high-temperature heat source and a source of highly concentrated sunlight for industrial process heat applications, material processing, and fuels and chemicals production. Although electric power production research and development continues, these nonelectric applications receive increasing consideration.

Parabolic trough systems concentrate onto a receiver running along the line-focus of a reflecting trough (Figure 5.3). Fresnel lens, linear systems are operationally much the same but use a lens to produce the line-focus. Trough systems generally track only in a single axis. Typical operating temperatures range from 90° C to 350° C. Trough systems are modular in nature and can provide process heat or drive a turbine-generator to produce electricity. Of the various medium- to high-temperature solar thermal technologies, trough systems are the most technically mature and commercially available. Such systems are being commercially marketed and privately financed today.

The Gould IPH (Industrial Process Heat) plant in Arizona is a 5,570-m^2 system of parabolic troughs supplying most of the 95° C hot water for industrial processing at the facility. It is a typical industrial process heat application using trough systems. Trough systems are also successfully being used for electric power generators. The Solar Energy Generating Station (SEGS) in California is a series of large trough systems producing power for sale to the Southern California Edison Company. SEGS 1 and 2 use 232,250 m^2 of collectors to produce 45 megawatts electric (MWe). A heat transfer oil is heated to 310° C (590° F) and used to generate saturated steam. Natural gas is then used to superheat the steam to 415° C. Both the Gould system and the SEGS plants are commercial, privately financed ventures.

Point-focus, or dish systems use two-axis tracking parabolic dishes to concentrate the sunlight to a receiver mounted at its focal point (Figure 5.4). The concentrated solar energy can heat a fluid circulating in the receiver. This heated fluid is then pumped for use or storage elsewhere. Heat engines can be mounted at the focal point and used to generate electricity, such as the system at Warren Springs, California. A single dish can achieve temperatures in excess of 1480° C and can produce up to 50 kilowatts electric (KWe). Dish systems, like troughs, are modular and can be combined in fields to generate large amounts of electricity or process heat.

The Solar Total Energy Project (STEP) in Georgia uses a field of 114 parabolic dishes and produces electricity and heat. The plant produces 400 kwe of electric power, 630 kilograms of 177° C steam and 231,300 kilograms of air-conditioning per day for use in a textile mill. A heat transfer fluid is heated to 399° C at the dish and is then pumped to a heat exchanger. Superheated steam drives a turbine-generator to produce electricity. Medium-pressure steam is extracted from the turbine for process steam, and the low-temperature steam from the turbine exhaust is used to run a chiller for air-conditioning.

A privately funded dish system in California, Solar Plant I, uses a 700-dish system to produce 4.4 MWe. Each dish is made up of 24 polymer-film parabolic mirrors each 1.5 meters in diameter. Another dish system, the Vanguard, mounts a Sterling engine in the focal point of a 10.8-meter-diameter dish to generate 25 kwe from a single dish. This system has achieved nearly a 30 percent net conversion efficiency.

The solar salt-gradient pond, or solar pond, has the unique advantage of utilizing a water problem--brine--to provide energy needed for water reclamation efforts. A solar pond (Figure 5.5) is a body of saline water generally 2 to 5 meters deep that acts as large solar collector and storage device. All ponds absorb solar energy striking them and heat up. In a conventional pond, the warm water rises and loses its heat at the surface by convection and evaporation. The solar pond suppresses the convection of warm water to the surface by the establishment of a stable density gradient.

A solar pond is made of three distinct zones. The surface convecting zone is a thin, top layer of low-salinity water that freely mixes. The second zone is the nonconvecting, salt-gradient zone. This layer, typically 1 to 1.5 meters thick, is established so that the concentration of salt increases with depth. As the concentration of salt increases, the density of the water increases, overwhelming the decrease in density that accompanies an increase in water temperature, thereby suppressing convection in this layer. The nonconvection zone acts as a thick layer of transparent insulation inhibiting convection losses from the bottom, storage layer.

The bottom zone is a mixed layer of high concentration of salt that acts as the thermal storage for the solar pond. This layer is typically 1 to 3.5 meters in depth. A large portion of the incident solar radiation is absorbed in the bottom storage layer and, by preventing convection losses, can reach substantial temperatures. Solar pond bottom thermal storage zones can typically range from 80 to 110° C. Energy may be extracted from the bottom layer and used for process heat or to run a turbine for electric power generation. Surface water from the cool, upper convection zone can act as a source of cooling water. Thermal conversion efficiencies of 15 to 20 percent are typical. Solar pond developments have progressed quite far, driven primarily by twenty-five years of Israeli work. A 5-MW solar pond power plant in Israel went on line in 1983, operating day and night.

Solar thermal technologies have made impressive gains over the last few years. These major new technologies have matured in record time. In 1973 the power tower concept in the United States was represented by little more than a "shaving mirror and toy boiler" bench-scale demonstration model. In less than ten years, the technology progressed to the point that a successfully operating 10 MWe pilot plant now exists. The central receiver heliostats fell from $900/m^2 for the Solar One 10-MWe plant to less than $100/m^2 in 1986. Stressed-membrane heliostats under development are expected to reduce that cost to less than $40/m^2, or one-twentieth of the cost of the Solar One heliostats. The dishes of the STEP system, designed in 1980 and constructed in 1982, had a concentration ratio of 235 and cost $1,000/m^2. The Solar Plant I dishes in 1986, with a concentration ration of 1,000, cost about $160/m^2. Parabolic trough systems being installed in 1979 at $2,300/kwt (kilowat thermal) dropped to about $760/kwt in 1986.

As is shown in Figure 5.6, the total costs of solar thermal capacity have dropped dramatically in the last seven years. From over $3,000/kwt in 1979 to less than $800/kwt in 1986 for heat production and from $7,000/kwe in 1980 to about $3,000/kwe in 1986 for electric power production, solar thermal systems are well on track to general cost-competitiveness. The U.S. Department of Energy's goals for the mid-1990s for solar thermal systems are summarized in Table 5.1. For process heat systems, the expected costs are $7-$9/MkJ (megakilojoules) and about $270 to $430/kwt. Electric power production systems are expected to drop to about 4-5 cents/kwhe or $1,000 to $1,200/kwe. Utility estimates for central receivers using the latest technologies are already as low as 7.8 cents/kwhe (kilowat hours of electricity). As with photovoltaic systems, solar thermal systems now offer cost advantages for specific matches of sites and needs and offer great potential for large-scale, widespread use for the next decade.

Solar thermal systems can provide electric power. Solar ponds and troughs can provide a medium-grade heat, whereas dishes and towers can provide high-grade heat and high concentrations of solar energy. Simpler solar systems, such as flat-plate collectors and solar stills, can be used for lower-grade, lower-temperature applications. Advanced concentrator systems can produce ultra-high concentrations, 10,000 suns and above, which may provide unique opportunities for photoreactions and material processing. The question, then, is: How may these technologies be used effectively to provide the energy to drive water reclamation efforts?

SOLAR DESALINATION

When considering solar applications to water reclamation, desalination is often the first option thought of and an area in which much effort has taken place. Solar desalination is a real option for the production of high-value potable water in areas of severe potable water scarcity and high-cost power. It is not currently considered an option for the bulk water requirements of conventional agriculture.

In a locality in which potable water is needed, one would consider the use of solar distillation if the following conditions were met:

1. Saline or brackish water is available.
2. A population is living in an arid area in which inexpensive, conventional sources of energy are not readily available.
3. Natural sources of fresh water under the control of the local population are not easily exploitable.
4. For extended periods of time, there is an adequate level of solar radiation intensity and reasonably high ambient temperatures.
5. Land is available and has little opportunity cost.

Solar desalination techniques may conveniently be considered in two broad categories: small-scale desalination by solar stills and large-scale desalination plants.

Solar-Still Desalination

The solar still employs simple, low-temperature solar thermal techniques to mimic the natural hydrologic cycle and to extract fresh water from saline or brackish water. The basic solar still (Figure 5.7) consists of a shallow water basin enclosed by a transparent cover. The basin is blackened on the surface to ensure maximum absorption of solar radiation for effective heating of the water. As the water is heated, water vapor is produced. The transparent and vapor-tight enclosure permits radiation to enter, prevents the escape of the humid air, acts as a radiation shield in reducing energy loss as a result of the long-wave radiation from the water surface, and provides a relatively cool surface on which part of the humidity can condense. Glass or certain plastic sheet materials are used for this transparent cover. The inner surface of the cover remains sufficiently cool to serve as the condenser. The water vapor condensing on the cover is then collected in troughs as freshwater product.

Desalination by solar stills is not really a new process; its principles were known to the ancients. T. A. Lawand reports that the Arabs used iron containers for operating certain desalination techniques using the sun.[3] The first reference of the possibility of solar desalination was made by the Italian Nicolo Ghezzi, who wrote a short treatise on the subject in 1742.[4] The first significant installation was made in Chile in 1872, as reported by Harding.[5] This solar still was a glass-covered installation that covered a ground area of 4,500 square meters and produced a maximum of some 19,000 liters per day of fresh water.

In 1973, Delyannis prepared a comprehensive inventory summarized by M. G. Latif, as shown in Table 5.2.[6] It is evident from this inventory that solar distillation has been tried on a fairly extensive basis in a number of different areas and climatic regions. As Table 5.2 also shows, nearly all large-size solar stills in operation as of 1973 were glass-covered. It seems that plastic as covers of large stills had not lasted as long as previously anticipated.

Although the cost of solar-distilled water cannot be appraised with certainty, depending on a variety of local factors, data based on nearly a dozen large solar stills in four countries (United States, Spain, Greece, and Australia) have permitted some usable cost estimates.[7] Basin-type solar stills of durable materials can be built in sizes of thousands of square meters at a cost of

74

$6.60-$22.0 per square meter. At these costs and with typical productivities, amortization rates, and other operating costs, solar-distilled water can be produced in favorable climates for $11-$22 per cubic meter ($3-$6 per 1,000 gallons). The same product water can be mixed with lower-quality water or with rainwater, if available, to produce an acceptable product of lower cost.

There are now large (millions of gallons per day) commercial plants desalting seawater at costs of $3.80/m^3, and designs of very large conventional plants anticipate total water production costs dropping to $1.90/m^3. It is clear that solar-still desalination in its current form cannot compete with these large desalting plants for such large production capabilities. On the other hand, the operation of these conventional systems with an output as low as 500 m^3/day would be extremely expensive. Cost analysis has shown that at capacity levels below 600 m^3/day an estimated cost of $11/m^3 for solar-still desalination is lower than the cost achieved by any other existing process when operating on seawater in a locality in which power supplies have to be specially provided. The vapor compression process is now the closest competitor to solar desalination in the 600-m^3/day-or-less capacity range.

In general, desalination by solar stills should be provided in quantities less than 20 cubic meters per day. This does not necessarily mean, however, that only small populations could be supported. Given that a human being can survive easily on approximately 10 liters of fresh water per day for basic needs, 2,000 persons per community could be supported on a 20-cubic-meter-per-day plant. For larger production, large-scale solar desalination plants should be considered.

The prime advantages of solar still distillation are: the use of locally available material; the use of a local labor force to undertake all the principal jobs in constructing, installing, operating, and maintaining the system; and a cost of operation that is not high if the unit has been appropriately constructed.

Large-Scale Solar Distillation

Major efforts to improve the efficiency of the solar stills were carried out in the 1960s, with some efforts continuing in the 1980s. These attempts to increase solar-still efficiency, however, have been limited to the rather narrow capabilities of conventional still components. These attempts have only made marginal improvement in solar-still efficiency, which continues to be about 30 percent.

Although solar stills can prove cost-effective for areas requiring modest production of water and are simple enough to maximize the use of local resources, much of the current effort is focused on large-scale distillation plants, which may be solar-powered or solar-assisted or may use conventional energy sources. These desalination processes include multi-effect plants, reverse osmosis (RO), and electrodialysis.

In a conventional solar still, the three basic processes of energy collection, evaporation, and condensation take place in the same unit. However, these processes can be separated and carried out in three different units in order to increase the yield for large-scale solar distillation systems. The efficiency of energy utilization is increased because of the control over the evaporation and condensation operations.

One major approach is the multi-effect humidification-dehumidification technique. The system, suggested by Garg et al., used a solar collector of 11–14 m^2 in which the brine is heated to 55–60° C and then circulated to a packed tower (humidifier) in which humidification of an air stream blown from the bottom takes place in contact with the hot brine stream sprayed over the top in counter current.[8] The humidification unit is connected with a surface condenser. Such a relatively small unit gave 61.25 liters per day.

A similar procedure was suggested by Ivekovic in 1976, in which conventional still-hot brine was drained into an evaporator to saturate air blown upward, then condensed in a condenser using saline water as a coolant.[9] Ivekovic reports that it is possible to increase markedly the amount of distilled water using these techniques.

An experimental solar distillation plant using a multiple-effect humidification-dehumidification process was built in Sonora, Mexico.[10] This installation was designed to produce 790-1,320 m^3/day, using a multiple-stage humidifier-dehumidifier designed to operate 24 hours per day with hot water from a storage tank. This water was heated partly by solar energy and partly by heat collected from the condensate. As indicated in Figure 5.8, seawater entered the condenser at 26° C, is heated therein to 61° C, and finally is heated to 66° C by passing through a solar heat collector. The solar collectors were double-glazed, with one piece of transparent plastic in contact with the water surface to prevent evaporation and a second plastic sheet held above the first by air inflation. Evaporation in the packed tower takes place as a result of humidification of air, which is circulated through the packing by a blower in the bottom cross-convention between the condenser and the packed tower. Ultimate failure of the plastic glazing finally forced the abandonment of the solar portion of this plant.

Another multi-effect technique is to use hot water or steam from solar concentrators to operate a multistage flash distiller, thus supplying the primary energy for operation. Weihe proposed a design of a pilot plant for the production of 1 metric ton of fresh water per hour using this technique.[11] The distiller was presumed to be kept running around the clock. Therefore, the collected solar energy must be stored for use during the night. The stored hot water was contained in a steel accumulator.

Moustofa, Jarrar, and El-Mansy describe a 10,000-liter solar multistage flash desalination system that was designed and tested at Kuwait Institute for Scientific Research.[12] The system consisted of a 200-m^2 solar-line-concentrating collector field, a 7,000-liter thermal storage tank, and a self-regulating 12-stage multistage flash desalination subsystem. The collector field, equipped with a closed-loop tracking system, was installed with individual troughs oriented in the north-south direction. An important consideration when comparing the potential multi-effect system output to that of the best-designed solar still becomes clear: This system can produce over ten times the output of the solar still for a given area of solar collector.

Another approach is reported by Badawi W. Tleimat, in which solar energy is used instead of fossil fuel to generate steam to drive a multi-effect distillation plant.[13] The scheme was optimized on the basis of minimum water cost using a solar boiler with an average daily output of 45,400 kg of saturated steam at 60 ^{o}C. Using a high performance evaporator-condenser, developed at the Sea Water Conversion Laboratory at the University of California, Berkeley, the result was optimum water costs ranging from $1.40 to $3.70 per m^3 for brackish water feed and $2.15 to $4.70 per m^3 for seawater feed. Under these conditions, the daily productivity per unit area of solar collectors ranged from 45 to 130 liters per m^2, depending on insolation and feedwater salinity. This is ten to forty times the average productivity of simple solar stills.

The wide variety of alternative techniques were reported under the Soleras program, a joint U.S.-Saudi Arabian solar energy venture.[14] These techniques varied widely. For example, Catalytic, Inc., designed a system using two 200-kw wind turbine-generators and 1,500 square meters of solar collector surface area (line-focus parabolic-trough solar collectors). The solar collectors drive a 35 kw organic turbine. This total installed capacity of 435 kw is used to drive a two-state reverse osmosis pump (low- and high-pressure stages) to desalinate 100 m^3/day of water with recovery factor of 90 percent. The cost estimates for larger systems range from $8.59/$m^3$ for 1,000 m^3/day to $5.65/$m^3$ for 10,000-m^3/day plants.

A Boeing Company pilot plant for desalinating 244 m^3/day employed a four-train reverse osmosis desalination unit powered primarily by solar thermal energy from an array of 436 point-focus heliostat collectors having a total area of 20,448 square meters. The heliostats direct the sun's rays to a 68-meter central receiver in which pressurized air, heated while flowing through heat-exchanger tubes, is used to power a 713-kw gas turbine electric generator unit operating on the Brayton cycle. The estimated costs for this design range from $4.95/m^3 for 1,000 m^3/day to $2.55/m^3 for 10,000-m^3/day production.

The Donavan, Hamester and Rattin, Inc., desalination system conceptual design is a hybrid of reverse osmosis and electrodialysis processes. Alternating-current power is generated for the reverse osmosis stage of the design by a power system employing line-focus solar thermal collectors and a turbine-generator operating on an organic rankine cycle. Direct current power for the electrodialysis stage of the desalination system is produced directly from a solar photovoltaic field and by AC/DC conversion. The Exxon and Martin Marietta subcontractor optimized-pilot plant system, the design of which was completed in May 1982, has an average daily water production rate of 272 m^3/day. The heliostats power a 54-kw electric turbine-generator unit by heating, at the top of a 37-meter central receiver, a working fluid consisting of molten salt, which in turn produces steam in a steam generator. Thermal storage capacity amounts to 13.5 megawatt-hours thermal, or roughly 28 hours of operability. One hundred percent of the plant's average needs would be met solely from solar resources. Peak power needs, however, would be met by supplemental electricity from the local utility grid. The plant would produce the product water at $7.75/m^3 for 5,000 m^3/day production.

These examples, and many others, indicate that a solar-powered distillation plant--that is, applying conventional flash distillation technique or any other known or well developed technique like reverse osmosis or electrodialysis--is a viable option. Future improvements will make these desalination plants even more cost-effective.

UTILIZING SOLAR POWER FOR WATER RECLAMATION SYSTEMS

Whether for large-scale desalination projects, wastewater treatment, water pumping, or other conventional water reclamation projects, photovoltaic or solar thermal electric power technologies can supply the power required. The selection of power sources for conventional water projects is based on site-specific economics. As solar technologies improve in cost-effectiveness, the range of economical applications expands. The water reclamation planner needs to consider and reevaluate solar power on the basis of the most up-to-date information possible and the real costs over the life of the project for the specific site involved. Through the 1990s, the relative economics of solar and conventional sources may be expected to continue to shift.

Solar Ponds: Problems Turned Solutions

Many water reclamation projects not only require large amounts of energy but result in a considerable amount of reject, highly concentrated brine. One possible solution to both problems is the coupling of solar ponds to desalination projects. Desalination projects produce large volumes of concentrated brine that is typically diverted to evaporation ponds and is little more than an undesirable waste product. Much of the cost of constructing a solar pond lies in the excavation and lining of the ponds and the cost of the salt. Much of this cost is already embedded in the cost of evaporative ponds and waste-brine disposal. The use of the waste brine to establish power-producing solar ponds represents a desirable trend toward synergy. The U.S. Bureau of Reclamation performed an excellent study on the establishment of solar ponds in the Southwest and their coupling to desalination projects.[15] According to this study, coupling of solar ponds to desalination projects allow:

* brine reject from the desalting plant to be used for solar pond construction;
* energy produced by the solar ponds to power the desalting process;
* intercepted brine from salinity-control projects to be used to construct solar ponds, thereby displacing significant portions of a disposal pond system.

The brine reject from the desalting plant can provide the surface flush for the solar ponds and, with further concentration, can provide the make-up for the storage layer.

Desalination waste may be reduced, as the power-producing solar ponds displace the need for a portion of the brine-disposal evaporation-pond area. The coupling of solar ponds to use reject brine also reduces the cost of power production by the solar pond. The solar pond with its integral thermal storage makes available to the desalination project a continuous source of electric power. The additional availability of thermal energy provides additional flexibility in the choice of desalination techniques.

The U.S. Bureau of Reclamation studied two specific desalination approaches coupled with solar ponds for the southwest.[16] Reverse osmosis desalination plants provide a good match with solar ponds. The thermal heat from the solar pond is used to run a rankine cycle to produce the mechanical energy needed to drive the very high pressure RO feed pumps. The second approach, horizontal-tube multi-effect (HTME) distillation also promises a good coupling with solar ponds, using the heat from the pond to generate 70° C to 82° C steam to drive a series of distillation effects. In addition, solar ponds can drive organic rankine engines to provide electrical energy for processing. As is shown by the data in Table 5.3, the cost savings over conventional sources may be substantial if the conventional sources need to be specifically provided on a dedicated basis.

In many areas, the need to control the flow of saline water into rivers requires the diversion and pumping of brine sources over large distances to evaporation ponds. Often, these remote areas have no surplus of available energy to operate the pumps. The coupling of solar ponds to salinity-control diversion projects in order to operate the needed pumps offers another useful match.

SOLAR ENHANCED WATER RECLAMATION

Solar thermal technologies may be applied to water reclamation and toxic waste destruction. The few examples included here suggest that far greater efforts would be appropriate in the future.

Solar-Catalyzed Ozone Reactor

Toxic organic compounds in our drinking water supplies, groundwater, and wastewater pose a substantial challenge to water treatment efforts. Compounds such as pesticides, methylene chloride, trichloroethylene (TCE), trialomethanes (THMs), perchloroethylene (PCE), and polychlorinated biphenyles (PCBs) are of increasing concern. Traditional water treatment processes have a variety of disadvantages. Disposal in landfills merely moves and postpones the problem and poses substantial threats to groundwater supplies. Activated carbon or reverse osmosis treatments simply concentrate the problem. Air-stripping transfers the problem from one medium to another, and appropriate biological treatments are often difficult to operate or inadequate under the wide variety of conditions that exist. Such toxins can be successfully destroyed, however, by using ozone as a powerful oxidizing regime that breaks down the toxic organics to harmless end products, such as carbon dioxide and water.[17]

Although ozone has been used for years in disinfection, odor control, the production of potable water, and for other purposes, its use to break down such organic toxins has been limited, in general because of the extremely slow reaction rates involved. Ozone is a powerful oxidant capable of oxidizing virtually all of the organic chemicals listed on the Environmental Protection Agency (EPA) Priority Pollutant List. The degree of oxidation, stoichiometric, and kinetic responses are, however, unacceptably low in some cases.

It has been demonstrated that the controlled combination of ozone and ultraviolet (UV) light produces rapid reactions in the form of rapid photochemical oxidation of halogenated organic compounds.[18] Ozone decomposition to free radicals is accelerated by absorption of ultraviolet light. Free radicals, having a considerably higher oxidation potential than molecular ozone, produce favorable reaction conditions with many of the hazardous organics found in groundwater. The reaction rates of UV/ozone processes can greatly exceed those of ozone oxidation alone. Figures 5.9 and 5.10 demonstrate the reaction rate advantages for a variety of cases.[19]

The need to accelerate reaction rates is clearly illustrated by consideration of such cases as DBCP (1,2-dichloro,3-chloropropane). The use of UV to accelerate the reaction is also justified by a consideration of the high cost of ozone and the need to reduce the amount of oxidant required. The production of ozone is very energy-intensive, requiring approximately 5.4 kwh of electrical energy per kilogram of ozone produced. Thus, the advantage of using a UV catalyst to accelerate the reaction and conserve ozone is great. The current method of introducing UV light into the process with UV lamps is itself, however, quite energy-intensive; often as much energy is required to operate the lamps as is saved by a reduction in ozone demanded by the reaction. The UV portion of the solar spectrum, when presented in concentrated form, would serve quite well and present definite opportunities for energy savings. Work is being done at the University of Arizona investigating such systems. Some questions about solar-catalyzed ozone reactors need to be resolved: design; whether any screening of the non-UV portion of the spectrum is desirable; and how to quantify optimum utilization of solar energy.

Solar-Enhanced Air-Stripping of Volatile Organic Chemicals in Groundwater

Air-stripping is a process for the removal of volatile organic chemicals (VOCs). The process is strongly affected by water and air temperatures. Increased mass transfer coefficients can be realized if solar-enhanced stripping processes are designed. There are no data available to evaluate the viability of this proposed process. This is particularly true for dispersed well-fields contaminated with VOCs. Enhancement of the air-stripping process by solar means needs to be evaluated in bench-scale and pilot-scale studies.

Thermally Enhanced Biological Detoxification of Priority Pollutants

The objective of groundwater reclamation can be the removal of toxicity. Chlorinated organics represent about 80 percent of the compounds classified as priority pollutants in 1986 and are primarily agents of toxic responses in animals and humans. A common subset of this class are chlorinated phenols. Detoxification of these compounds involves the cleavage of all the chlorine groups from the carbon ring structure. The process has been observed in aerobic environments, but there is concern that intermediates of increased toxicity are formed at points in the reaction sequence. Improper control of the treatment system could increase environmental hazard. Detoxification of chlorinated phenols has also been observed under anaerobic conditions, but the rate of reaction is much slower. Anaerobic reactions are usually very sensitive to temperature, and the low temperature of groundwater is a major cause of the slow reaction rate. An advantage of anaerobic detoxification is a consistent, sequential decrease in toxicity as intermediates are produced. A major disadvantage has been the difficulty of achieving complete detoxification under anaerobic conditions.

Because aerobic and anaerobic reactions have unique advantages for detoxification, an anaerobic-aerobic treatment sequence has become a major focus of interest. Such a treatment scheme is difficult to implement in situ and would favor surface facilities. Once groundwater is brought to the surface for treatment, however, the rates of both aerobic and anaerobic reactions can be increased by solar heating of the water. Rates have been identified for mesophilic bacteria at temperatures up to 35° C, but research has not yet defined the potential enhancement of pertinent reaction rates using thermophilic bacteria in 55° C reactors. Solar heating may make the surface detoxification of polluted groundwater much more economically feasible by significantly increasing the rate of reaction in anaerobic-aerobic units.

SOLAR DETOXIFICATION OF HAZARDOUS WASTE

Many of our most important surface and groundwater supplies have increasingly become contaminated with a veritable alphabet soup of toxic chemicals. There are a number of strong indications that the application of direct solar flux can lead to the detoxification of a variety of hazardous wastes. The UV portion of the spectrum is of particular importance in many of these reactions, as is the level of flux. Many of these reactions may also require high temperatures that would be generated by a high-concentration system, whereas some of them proceed at lower temperatures. Several possible approaches have been identified by the Solar Thermal Division of the Solar Energy Research Institute (SERI); summaries of these follow.[20]

Catalyzed Photodecomposition Using Direct Solar Flux

Concentrated solar thermal energy can be directly absorbed in water containing a photoactive catalyst to photodecompose toxic organic pollutants to benign chemicals. These benign chemicals may then either be removed by further processing or remain in the resulting potable water. The detoxification proceeds by a mechanism of photochemical or photoelectrochemical oxidation of the pollutants by photons, which are present in the concentrated sunlight.[21] This effect has potential use as the basis for a commercial process to renovate contaminated water.

Experiments sponsored by SERI demonstrated the feasibility of decomposing the organics phenol and p-chloratoluene in aqueous streams using simulated sunlight at fluxes up to 5 suns and in the presence of catalytic titanium dioxide. Those rudimentary experiments showed that increasing the flux increased the rate of photo-oxidation and that the rate is highly dependent upon the particular organic pollutant and upon the specific catalyst.[22] Analysis of the existing literature shows that other researchers have also experimentally demonstrated the feasibility of photodecomposing other organic compounds in water at a wide range of solar flux levels.[23] As discussed earlier, some existing pollution abatement processes use ultraviolet lamps.[24] The U.S. Army at the Edgewood Arsenal tested the lamps to be used for the oxidation of nitro derivatives of benzene (e.g., trinitrotoluene), which were present in water at the level of 100 to 200 parts per million (ppm). The army's experience with electrically powered lamps was less than satisfactory, because of the high cost of electricity and because of the short lamp life.

This type of situation is ideal for the direct application of concentrated sunlight. A typical process would use the direct flux to decontaminate the water when the sun is shining. The products of the decontamination may range from water and carbon dioxide, for a simple organic containing only carbon and hydrogen atoms, to other products such as hydrochloric acid, for chlorinated compounds. In many cases, it is conceivable that no additional treatment would be required to produce recyclable water. A secondary treatment might be necessary in other cases, depending upon the products of the photodecomposition and their concentrations and whether the water was to be used for human consumption.

The contact of the catalyst, contaminated water, and sunlight may be carried out on either a continuous or a batch basis when the sun is shining. The catalyst might be a simple and inexpensive compound, such as titanium dioxide, that can be discarded after use. It might also be a precious metal, which would require recycling. The catalyst could be a granular solid, which is removed from the water by simple filtration. It is important to realize that the detoxification process may be carried out in batches whenever the sun is shining and does not need to be continuous. The contaminated water can be stored when the sun is not shining for later processing at a high rate when the sun does shine. This process requires no energy storage but rather storage of the water in simple ponds or tanks.

The solar decomposition of organics in water can be combined with other processes to form an efficient and cost-effective hybrid procedure having the best characteristics of each individual process. An example might be a solar photodecomposition process followed by a carbon adsorption process. The bulk of the organic would be removed or transformed by the solar thermal oxidation process, and the balance would be removed by a serial bed of activated carbon. This type of hybrid process should be very efficient and would still reap the benefits of doing the bulk of the detoxification by using solar thermal energy.

High-Flux Direct Solar Incineration

High-temperature incineration is the standard disposal method for many of the most hazardous toxic organic wastes. High-temperature incinerators consume large amounts of fossil fuels and suffer from short service life and maintenance problems because of the high temperatures required. Not only could solar detoxification save fossil fuel, but through the proper match of spectral distribution of concentrated sunlight to the organic compound involved, it can greatly reduce the temperature requirements and associated problems.[25] For the decomposition to take place, an activation energy barrier must be overcome. For complex organic molecules, this activation energy may be on the order of 40 to 90 Kcal/mole (kilocalories per mole). As shown in Figure 5.11, a 15 Kcal/mole reduction in activation energy can reduce the temperature required by 600° C. Thus, as Graham and Dellinger state, "altering the activation energy is a powerful means of increasing destruction efficiency."[26]

A photoquantum reaction may be employed to

87

accomplish this. As shown in Figure 5.12, if the molecule absorbs radiation of sufficient energy, an excited state can be achieved. A particular band of wavelengths will be most effective. Although the first excited state may not be stable in the high temperature environment of an incinerator, the first state may decay to a metastable triplet state. The activation energy for decomposition of this state is much less than for the ground state and even less than for the first excited state. The ultraviolet-visible portion of the solar spectrum alters the electronic state of organic compounds so that much less energy is required to destroy them than in conventional incineration processes. Another attractive feature of a solar incineration process is that when the heat is supplied by an external radiant source rather than by a chemical combustion source, the need for excess oxygen is greatly reduced, which will also significantly reduce cost. Also, a solar source will eliminate the production of soot, which is a major problem in conventional incinerators. A flux concentration on the order of 1,000 suns will rapidly destroy any soot while increasing the efficiency of heat absorption.

The physical mechanisms that govern the various solar detoxification processes are not well known. Extensive investigation needs to be done to accumulate the detailed knowledge that will be necessary to scale up these processes. Also, engineering analyses should be initiated to determine the economics and identify the development necessary to scale up these processes to a commercial size.

Natural concern about preventing and eliminating hazardous-waste contamination is rising. Representative Bob Edgar, a ranking Democrat on the House Subcommittee on Water Resources, insists that pollution, particularly in groundwater, "is the issue for the 1980s and 1990s." We should increase our research effort to determine what potential we have for relieving a major national problem.

A CALL FOR ACTION

Great advances have taken place in solar technologies since the 1970s, leading to major cost reductions that continue. As the relative economics of solar and conventional energy sources shift, the arena in which solar can successfully compete for powering water reclamation systems expands and requires constant reevaluation. More important, there exists, in 1986 and in the next 5 to 10 years, a wide variety of site-specific applications in which a favorable model may exist between water processing needs, lack of low-cost power, and the solar resource. In addition, solar offers a number of opportunities that can take advantage of some of the unique properties of the solar resource.

Solar development in 1988 is severely hampered by the low level of funds for research, development, and demonstration of the new generation of solar technologies. Water reclamation and toxic-waste destruction to protect our water supplies is fast becoming a priority of national and international concern. Of the billions of dollars being committed for water quality, supply, and protection, there exists a very real synergistic opportunity to invest a small fraction in our future by supporting the development of solar technologies applied to water reclamation. This will not only help to identify potential long-term energy savings resulting in lower water project costs but will stimulate solar development in general, continuing the advances needed to make solar more cost-effective. By focusing on the specific niches in which solar technologies may find early application to water problems, we can expand our options for water while providing the vital push needed for the next stage of solar development.

We propose that a Solar Thermal Water Reclamation Research Center be established to focus research, development, and demonstration efforts on the niches that exist for solar application to water problems. A modest, ongoing, coordinated effort now will permit solar to play a role in providing solutions to water problems in a timely fashion. It will also provide a much-needed boost for current solar efforts.

NOTES

1. L. Awerbuch, "U.S. Policy Structure on Middle East and North African Water Resources," Remarks at Conference on U.S. Foreign Policy on Water Resources in the Middle East and the Horn of Africa, Center for Strategic and International Studies, Washington, D.C., 20 February 1986.
2. Solar Thermal Power, SP-273-3043, SERI (Solar Energy Research Institute), Golden, Colo., 1987.
3. T. A. Lawand, "Systems for Solar Distillation," Presented at the International Conference for Appropriate Technologies for Semi Arid Areas: Wind and Solar Energy for Water Supply, Berlin-West, 15-20 September 1975.
4. Ibid.
5. J. Harding, "Apparatus for Solar Distillation," Proceedings of Institute of Civil Engineers, vol. 73, pp. 284-288, 1983.
6. A. Delyannis and E. Delyannis, "Solar Distillation Plants of High Capacity," 4th International Symposium on Fresh Water from the Sea, vol. 4, pp. 487-491, 1973.
7. M. G. Latif, "Solar Desalination," M.Sc. Thesis, El Minia University, Egypt, 1983.
8. S. K. Garg et al., "Development of Humidification-Dehumidification Technique for Water Desalination in Arid Zones of India," 2nd European Symposium on Fresh Water from the Sea, Athens, 9-12 May 1987.
9. H. Ivekovic, "Water by Dehumidification of Air Saturated with Vapor Below 80° C," 5th International Symposium on Fresh Water from the Sea, vol. 2, pp. 456-457, 1976.
10. C. N. Hodges et al., Solar Distillation Using Multiple-Effect Humidification, Office of Saline Water Research and Development Progress Report #194, U.S. Department of the Interior, Washington, D.C., 1966.
11. H. Weihe, "Fresh Water from Sea Waters: Distilling by Solar Energy," Solar Energy, vol. 13, pp. 439-444, 1972.
12. S. M. A. Moustofa, D. I. Jarrar, and H. I. El-Mansy, "Performance of a Self-Regulating

Solar Multistage Flash Desalination System," <u>Solar Energy</u>, vol. 35, no. 4, pp. 333-340, 1985.

13. B. W. Tleimat, "Optimal Water Cost from Solar Powered Distillation of Saline Water," <u>Proceedings Baghdad Conference</u> (1-6 December 1981), pp. 459-489.

14. Midwest Research Institute, <u>SOLERAS</u>, Kansas City, Mo., 1986.

15. W. J. Boegli, M. M. Dahl, H. E. Remmers, <u>Southwest Region Solar Pond Study for Three Sites--Tularosa Basin, Malaga Bend, and Canadian River</u>, U.S. Department of the Interior, Denver, Colo., 1984.

16. Ibid.

17. D. B. Fletcher, "UV/Ozone Process Treats Toxics," <u>Waterworld News</u>, pp. 25-28, May/June 1987.

18. Ibid.

19. Ibid. An additional reference is H. W. Prengle, C. E. Mauk, and J. E. Payne, "Ozone/UV Oxidation of Chlorinated Compounds in Water," Forum on Ozone Disinfection, 2-4 June 1976, Chicago, Ill., International Ozone Institute.

20. J. Thornton, <u>Some Perspectives on the Potential for Solar Detoxification of Hazardous Wastes</u>, RI/MR-250-3122, SERI, Golden, Colo., 1987.

21. J. Cooper and A. Nozick, "Hydrogen Production Using Photocatalytic Semiconductor Powers and Colloids," SERI, Golden, Colo., 1985. An additional reference is D. F. Ollis, "Heterogeneous Photocatalysis for Water Purification:Prospects and Problems," North Carolina State University, Raleigh, N.C., 1984.

22. Cooper and Nozick, "Hydrogen Production Using Photocatalytic Semiconductor Powers and Colloids."

23. Ollis, "Heterogeneous Photocatalysis for Water Purification."

24. M. Roth and J. M. Murphy, <u>Ultraviolet-Ozone and Ultraviolet-Oxidant Treatment of Pink Water</u> (ARLLCD-TR-78057), U.S. Army Armament Research and Development Command, Dover, N.J., 1987. Additional references are B. Jackson and J. M. Lachowski, <u>Overview of Pink Water Treatment Technology at DARCOM Facilities</u> (AD-E401-132), U.S. Army Armament Research and Development Center, Dover, N.J., 1984, and R. Hewett,

"Preliminary Assessment of the Feasibility of Utilizing Solar Thermal Technology to Detoxify Pink Water," SERI, Golden, Colo., 1986.

25. J. L. Graham and R. Dellinger, <u>A Laboratory Evaluation of the Solar Incinerability of Hazardous Organic Wastes</u>, SERI Progress Report, University of Dayton, 1985. An additional reference is D. E. Osborn, <u>Spectrally Selective Beam Splitters Designed to Decouple Quantum and Thermal Solar Energy Conversion in Hybrid Concentrating Systems</u>, SERI Final Report (XK-4-04070-01), University of Arizona, Tucson, 1987.

26. Ibid.

TABLE 5.1
Solar Thermal Technologies Costs

	Electric Cost (1984 $)	Process Heat Cost (1984 $)
System Costs--Current		
Central Receiver	2,900/kwe	800/kwt
Dish	3,400/kwe	780/kwt
Trough		760/kwt
Energy Costs--Current		
Central Receiver	0.13/kwhe	21/MBtu
Dish	0.13/kwhe	17/MBtu
Trough		30/MBtu
System Costs--1990s Goal		
Central Receiver	1,000/kwe	270/kwt
Dish	1,200/kwe	430/kwt
Trough		370/kwt
Energy Costs--1990s Goal		
Central Receiver	0.04/kwhe	7/MBtu
Dish	0.05/kwhe	9/MBtu
Trough		9/MBtu

Source: U.S. Department of Energy, National Solar Thermal Technical Program, Five Year Research and Development Plan, 1986-1990, DOE/CE-0160, 1986.

TABLE 5.2
The Most Important Solar Still Distillation Plants
as of 1973

Country	Year	m^2	Cover	Remarks
Australia	1963	372	Glass	Rebuilt
	1966	372	Glass	Operating
	1966	3,160	Glass	Operating
	1966	372	Glass	Operating
	1966	557	Glass	Operating
	1967	413	Glass	Operating
Cape Verde Island	1965	743	Plastic	
	1968			Abandoned
Chile	1872	4,460	Glass	Abandoned
	1968	100	Glass	Operating
Greece	1964	2,686	Plastic	Rebuilt
	1968	2,600	Str. plast.	Dismantled
	1965	1,490	Plastic	Rebuilt
	1968	1,486	Str. plast.	Abandoned
	1965	388	Plastic	Abandoned
	1967	8,600	Glass	Operating
	1968	2,508	Glass	Operating
	1969	2,005	Glass	Operating
	1971	2,200	Glass	Operating
	1971	2,400	Glass	Operating
	1973	2,528	Glass	Operating
India	1965	377	Glass	Operating
Mexico	1969	95	Glass	Operating
Pakistan	1969	306	Glass	Operating
	1972	9,072	Glass	Operating
Spain	1966	868	Glass	Operating
Tunisia	1967	440	Glass	Operating
	1968	1,300	Glass	Operating

United States	1959	228	Glass	Rebuilt
	1961	246	Glass	Dismantled
	1961	216	Plastic	Dismantled
	1963	148	Plastic	Dismantled
USSR	1969	600	Glass	Operating
West Indies	1967	1,710	Plastic	Operating

Source: M. G. Latif, "Solar Desalination," M.Sc. Thesis, El Minia University, Egypt, 1983.

TABLE 5.3
Cost Summary of Single Purpose Desalination Plants

Cost of Product Water ($/m^3)

	Intermediate Local Power		Base Load Power	
	Solar Pond	Oil	Solar Pond	Coal
Reverse Osmosis				
20,000 m^3/day	$0.53-0.61	$0.72-0.86	$0.51-0.59	$0.61-0.66
200,000 m^3/day	$0.49-0.56	$0.68-0.82	$0.47-0.49	$0.57-0.62
HTME Distillation				
20,000 m^3/day	$0.85-1.00	$4.16-7.90	$0.82-0.94	$1.90-2.25
200,000 m^3/day	$0.68-0.83	$3.50-4.90	$0.65-0.80	$1.56-1.86

Source: After W. J. Boegli and M. M. Dahl, Southwest Region Solar Pond Study for Three Sites--Tularosa Basin, Malaga Bend, and Canadian River, U.S. Department of the Interior, Denver, Colo., 1984

Photo 5.1.   University of Arizona Ultra-high
Concentration Solar Facility, University of
Arizona Solar and Energy Research Facility.

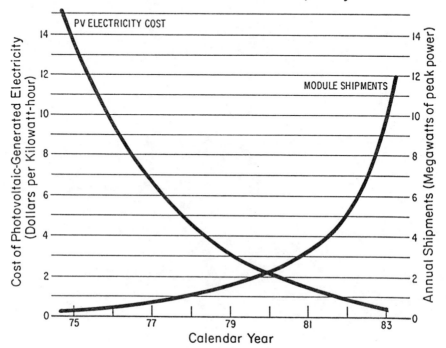

Cost of Photovoltaic Capacity

Figure 5.1.   U.S. Photovoltaic Costs and
Shipments.   U.S. Department of Energy,
Photovoltaic Energy Technology Division, <u>Five Year
Research Plan, 1984-1988, Photovoltaics:
Electricity from Sunlight</u>. DOE/CE-0072, 1983.

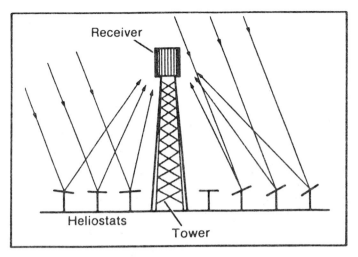

Figure 5.2. Power tower, or central receiving system. Solar Energy Research Institute, Golden, Colo.

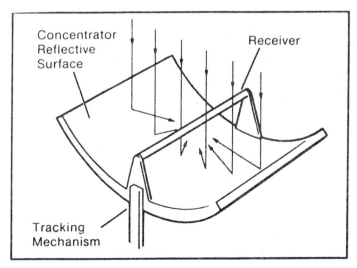

Figure 5.3. Parabolic trough system. Solar Energy Research Institute, Golden, Colo.

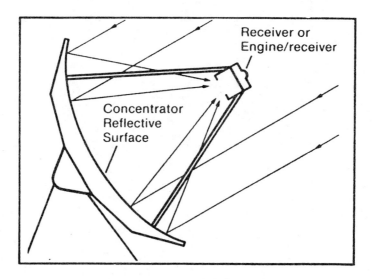

Figure 5.4. Point focus, or dish, system. Solar
Energy Research Institute, Golden, Colo.

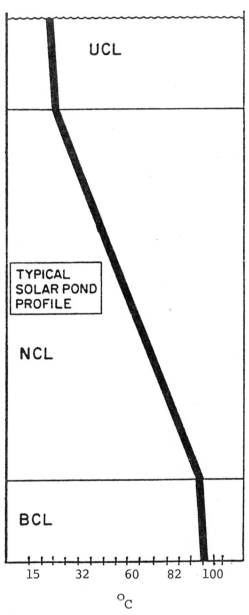

Figure 5.5. Solar salt-gradient pond. University of Arizona Solar and Energy Research Facility.

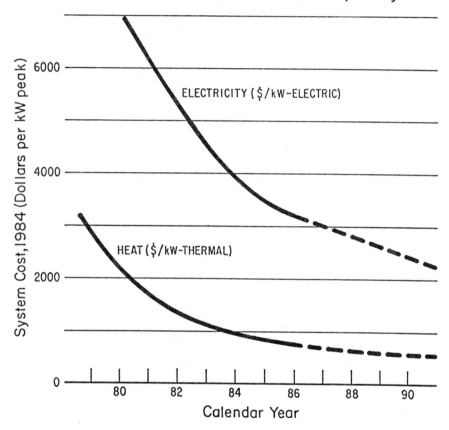

Figure 5.6. U.S. Solar Thermal Costs. U.S. Department of Energy, National Solar Thermal Technology Program, _Five Year Research and Development Plan, 1986-1990_. DOE/CE-0160, 1986

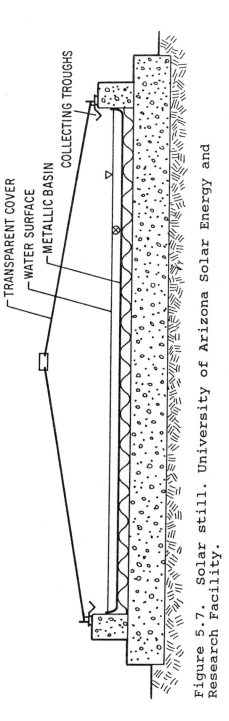

TRANSPARENT COVER
WATER SURFACE
METALLIC BASIN
COLLECTING TROUGHS

Figure 5.7. Solar still. University of Arizona Solar Energy and
Research Facility.

103

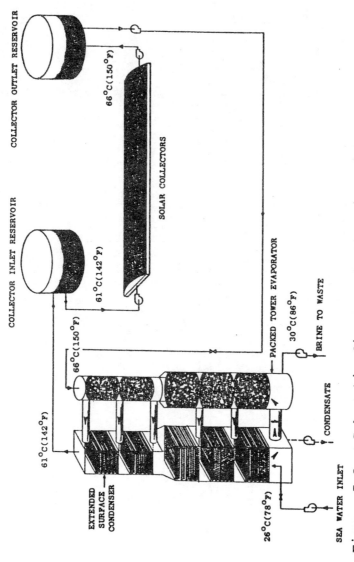

COLLECTOR OUTLET RESERVOIR

COLLECTOR INLET RESERVOIR

66°C(150°F)

61°C(142°F)

SOLAR COLLECTORS

66°C(150°F)

61°C(142°F)

PACKED TOWER EVAPORATOR

30°C(86°F)

BRINE TO WASTE

EXTENDED
SURFACE
CONDENSER

CONDENSATE

SEA WATER INLET

26°C(78°F)

Figure 5.8. Schematic diagram of the University of Arizona/University of Sonora solar desalination multiple-effect plant at Puerto Penasco, Sonora, Mexico. A. B. Meinel and M. P. Meinel, Applied Solar Energy: An Introduction (Addison Wesley Publishing Co., Reading, Mass. 1976): 557.

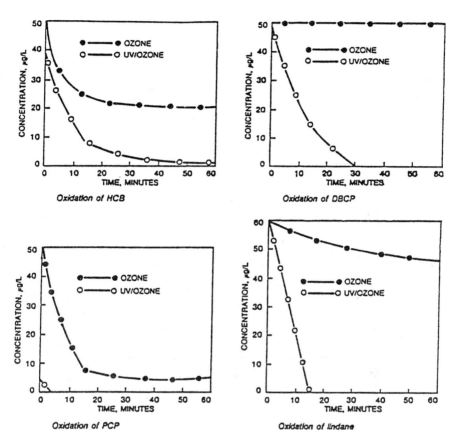

Figure 5.9. Photoenhanced-Ozone Toxic Organic Compound Decomposition Rates. After D. B. Fletcher, "UV/Ozone Process Treats Toxics," Waterworld News, pp. 25-28, May/June 1987.

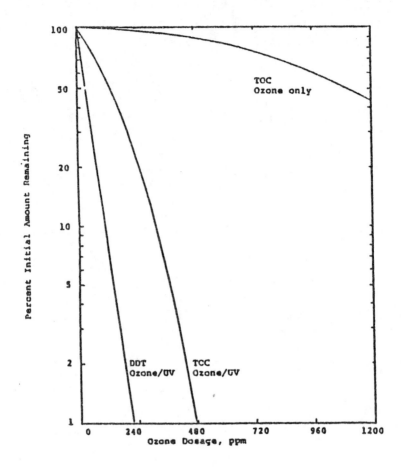

The Ozonation and Photo-oxidation of DDT
Initial concentration, 60 ppb.
Initial TOC, 16 ppm.

Figure 5.10. Photoenhanced-Ozone Decomposition of
Pesticides. Note the increased reaction rates for
the destruction of total organic carbons (TOC). H.
W. Prengle, C. E. Mauk and J. E. Payne, "Ozone/UV
Oxidation of Chlorinated Compounds in Water,"
Forum on Ozone Disinfection, June 2-4, Chicago,
Illinois, International Ozone Institute.

106

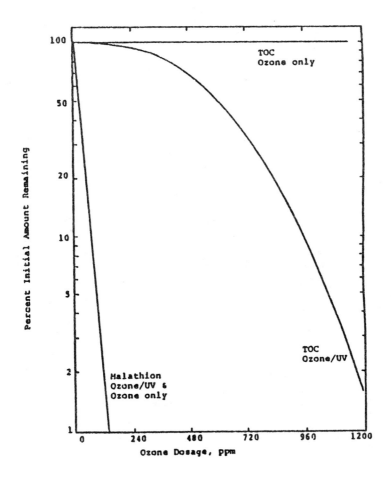

The Ozonation and Photo-oxidation of
Malathion.
Initial concentration, 55 ppm.
Initial TOC, 24 ppm.

Figure 5.10 (continued)

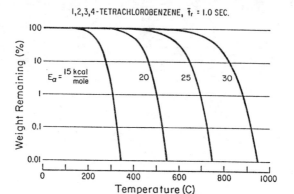

1,2,3,4-TETRACHLOROBENZENE, $\bar{t}_r$ = 1.0 SEC.

Figure 5.11. Computer Modeled Thermal Decomposition Profile for the Effect of Activation Energy. J. L. Graham and R. Dellinger, "A Laboratory Evaluation of the Solar Incinerability of Hazardous Organic Wastes," Solar Energy Research Institute Progress Report, University of Dayton, 1985.

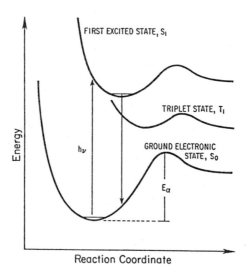

Figure 5.12. Energy vs. Reaction Coordinate Plot for the Overall Reaction of Hazardous Waste-to-Products. J. L. Graham and R. Dellinger, "A Laboratory Evaluation of the Solar Incinerability of Hazardous Organic Wastes," Solar Energy Research Institute Progress Report, University of Dayton, 1985.

6

Direct Seawater Irrigation as a Major Food Production Technology for the Middle East

Carl N. Hodges, Wayne L. Collins,
and James J. Riley

Food production requires sunlight, water, and land. The earth intercepts perhaps only one-half of one-billionth of the electromagnetic radiation from the continuously exploding sun, but this totals more than 400 trillion kilowatt hours per year. Water covers 71 percent of the surface of the planet; the oceans contain 1,320 million cubic kilometers, with more in the polar icecaps. There are millions of square kilometers of land with suitable soil.

Unfortunately, these conditions cannot always be utilized effectively for agriculture. Contemporary cultures, for example, are not adept at utilizing solar energy. In addition, the oceans and icecaps lock up more than 99 percent of all water, holding it unuseable or inaccessible. Finally, barely 3 percent of the land has climate sufficiently benign for crops--the rest is too hot or too cold, or too wet or too dry.

The most effective collectors and users of solar energy are green plants, through the marvelous chemistry of photosynthesis. The more sunlight, the more plant growth. Given water and suitable soils, desert regions could be the most productive croplands in the world, as they enjoy long hours of intensive sunlight.

Conventional agriculture requires large quantities of water. Plants are structured to permit the easy entry of carbon dioxide into the leaves. An unavoidable result of that is the even easier exit of water, because of the difference in concentration gradients between the gas and the liquid. Plants lose much more water than the amount of CO_2 they take in. This is true even of drought-resistant desert plants, which indeed are often the most profligate with water. Many quiescent desert species have evolved to take up CO_2 very rapidly when a rare rainstorm passes and water is available. They therefore lose water even more rapidly than do other plants in order to assimilate the gas.

Paradoxically, although deserts can be the most fecund of croplands if water is abundant, the very definition of a desert means that water is scarce. Only where major upland rivers pass through deserts en route to the sea does one find examples of the prodigious potentials: for example, the lower Nile, or southern California.

Desert seacoasts have been particularly frustrating for millennia. The land is empty and unused, and there are limitless amounts of water offshore. Here, in full measure, is all that is needed for maximum productivity: land, water, and sunlight. The dream of greening the desert with seawater is probably as old as agriculture itself. It has been tried repeatedly. To summarize a lengthy literature, however, classic food plants still wither and die at salinities far lower than that of seawater. This is not surprising. Because of geographic patterns of history, the food plants humans found and domesticated were freshwater plants.

Science has paid little attention to wild plants that tolerate salt water--plants that not only survive full-strength seawater but thrive on it. Terrestrial plants that tolerate various degrees of salt in the water are called halophytes. They evolved where available water was too salty for conventional plants. Some of them grow where they are irrigated only by the rise and fall of the tide. Fresh water dismays them, a rain makes them wilt.

The plants that thrive on seawater, and even require its high content of sodium chloride, are called euhalophytes. The salt they must accept in order to get water is stored separately in plant cells where it does not interfere with their metabolism. To reduce salt intake they have reduced water intake as well; they use water so efficiently and conserve it so well that they need only one-half to one-third as much water as do other plants.

With few exceptions, halophytes have been ignored by farmers and livestock because the plants often grow in uninhabited places. Also, many of them resemble unattractive weeds and are salty to the taste, although in remote regions of the Australian desert saltbush halophytes are sometimes grazed by stock, because little other forage is available.

On investigation, however, halophytes are proving to have astonishing characteristics. These include high yield, high protein, high-quality vegetable oil, and forage that does not always have to be desalted--or, when it does, is desalted simply and inexpensively. In addition, there is a spectrum of halophytes not useful for human or animal food but attractive as seawater-irrigated ornamental plants.

The Environmental Research Laboratory of the University of Arizona has been investigating these little-known plants for a decade. The effort began as one of several exercises to find a beneficial disposal of pumped seawater after it had been used and enriched by the on-shore culture of marine shrimp. We are convinced that ultimately a combined and almost symbiotic marine aquaculture and agriculture is inevitable.

Early success with halophyte specimens gathered casually from a small area of Mexico led to four years of collecting expeditions in the coastal and inland deserts of the planet. We now have what is believed to be the largest halophyte germ-plasm collection in the world, with more than a thousand acquisitions. In a long-term program, we are screening these for salt tolerance and usefulness, but we also began at once an accelerated domestication of some of the more-promising candidates.

HALOPHYTE CULTIVATION

Chief among the more promising halophyte candidates is a versatile oilseed crop we have

111

assigned the code name of SOS-7 (for the seventh year of intensive selection of the species). It is an improved strain of <u>salicornia</u>. We have been growing it for several years in demonstration farms in Mexico (Kino Bay, in Sonora) and in the United Arab Emirates (Sharjah and Abu Dhabi). It is now being commercialized by a new company, Halophyte Enterprises, which has funded much of the research.

SOS-7 is a seven-month crop, irrigated solely with seawater and requiring essentially conventional cultivating practices and farm machinery. The projected yield is 20 metric tonnes per hectare (MT/ha) of dried whole plant material. By comparison, alfalfa, which requires large quantities of fresh water, produces 5 to 20 MT/ha.

Of the total yield of 20 tonnes, 2 tonnes (10 percent) of this halophyte crop are oilseed. This seed contains no salt. Thirty percent of the seed (.6 of a tonne) is a high-quality vegetable oil for human consumption. The meal left over from the seed after oil extraction (1.4 tonnes) is a 43 percent-protein feed for livestock or poultry.

The remaining 18 tonnes of original plant material are straw containing about 7 tonnes of salt. Sixty-five percent of the salt is easily leached from the straw by soaking in seawater itself, followed by a brief rinse. This yields more than 13 tonnes of roughage suitable for livestock.

The vegetable oil is unusual for a product of a seawater-irrigated crop. The oil is extracted conventionally from SOS-7 seed by expeller or chemical solvent, similar to the processes used for soybean oil extraction. The characteristics of the oil were determined by our own analytical laboratory and separately by the laboratories of Archer Daniels Midland, the largest agricultural company in the United States.

Processed SOS-7 oil is most easily described as being virtually identical to safflower oil. It is high in linoleic acid, which means it is highly polyunsaturated, a characteristic now known to be desirable in human diets. University tests have shown that it substitutes easily for safflower oil or butter in all types of recipes, and its storage characteristics are similar to those of soybean oil. It can be partially hydrogenated to extend its shelf life.

Compared to other vegetable oils, the SOS-7 product has a relatively high chlorophyll content. If processed with only a single bleaching at the refinery, it has the appearance of olive oil. This may be a desirable marketing attribute in some regions, although a second bleaching can remove all color if desired.

Yet another use for this seawater-irrigated plant is as a forage crop. After harvesting, the oil-rich and nutritious seeds are not removed but, as with alfalfa, the whole plant is baled to be fed to livestock. In desert regions that import all forage, SOS-7 is actually much more valuable as an animal feed than as a source of vegetable oil.

To determine the efficacy of SOS-7 as a forage crop, a series of feeding trials has been conducted in the United States, Mexico, and the United Arab Emirates since 1983. These continuing trials have involved steers, goats, and sheep. Although generalizations are perilous, it appears as though steers fed comparable amounts of alfalfa and desalted halophyte in separate diets had the same weight gain. Goats and sheep have done very well with significant percentages of unwashed halophytes in their diet. In current trials in the UAE, goat diets consist of up to 100 percent washed or unwashed SOS-7 forage. This means a complete replacement of the freshwater-grown Rhodes grass now imported throughout the region.

Farm design and operation for the cultivation of SOS-7 are not dissimilar to that of other farms, except that the site must be near a seacoast, to provide for seawater intakes or wells. Other halophyte species may be more appropriate for inland regions with salinized soil or where only brackish groundwater is available.

Like any crop, the SOS-7 has specific requirements. It is a warm climate plant: it needs an air temperature constantly higher than 21° C during the last 120 days of its growing season. The temperature of the seawater used for irrigation must be, at the point of application, above 18° C. The amount of water required for the crop is approximately twice the local Potential Evaporation Rate. The crop is irrigated daily after seeding and less frequently as it matures. Although seawater and soil contain most plant nutrients, additional fertilizers such as nitrogen and phosphorus will increase the yield.

Land preparation is generally the same as for any flood-irrigated farm, and if there is a near-surface impeding layer in the soil a field drainage system may be required. Labor requirements are no different than those of similar field crops, and only general farm equipment and machinery are used. Our experience in Mexico and the Middle East suggests that the crop could be grown using manual labor and animal traction in lesser-developed areas.

Revenues for harvested material may be calculated by comparisons with existing regional prices. Vegetable oil, seed, meal, and straw are valued at the costs of comparable products, and animal fodder is usually priced on the basis of its protein or total nutritional content.

Use of seawater for irrigation should not turn the surface of the land salty. The ground surface does not accumulate salt from the seawater, as each successive irrigation carries the salts down with it. If the soil is highly permeable and there is no impeding layer, the salts are leached down below the root-growing zone of the plants. If there is low permeability, the fields require drainage ditches, and the excess salts are carried away with the drain water.

Also, seawater irrigation should not pollute a region's water table. The water table beneath a farm using seawater irrigation should be salty to begin with, or no such farming should be undertaken. No one is advised to attempt seawater irrigation of land overlying a freshwater aquifer. This technology is for desert seacoasts, where there is little or no freshwater groundwater.

In summary, then, the design, construction, operation, yield and revenue of a halophyte farm are roughly comparable to a well-managed conventional or freshwater forage farm in the same region.

What is significant, of course, is seawater irrigation. These crops not only produce food and

114

forage from land and water now unused and unuseable, but they also save large amounts of fresh water, which thereby become available for other, more beneficial uses.

The total world area available for halophyte production is difficult to state with precision. The combined length of the sparsely inhabited desert seacoasts of the world is probably between 20,000 and 40,000 kilometers. The width, or how far inland seawater farming is feasible (to a maximum elevation of 150 meters above mean sea level) probably averages at least several kilometers. Certainly the amount of coastal desert land available for halophyte production totals hundreds of thousands of square kilometers, or millions of hectares.

POSSIBLE LOCATIONS FOR HALOPHYTE CULTIVATION

What can be done in the way of halophyte cultuvation is highly site-specific. Here are some examples: India in 1986 imported approximately one-fourth of its vegetable oil--1.2 million tonnes per year--valued at $400 million. At the same time, 1.2 million hectares of once-fertile land near the Gulf of Kutch have become too salty for agriculture, because the over-pumping of groundwater for irrigation permitted seawater intrusion. Wells have now turned brackish, which in turn has impoverished more than a million people in 800 villages.

Two million hectares of the halophyte SOS-7, half of which could be grown in that salinized region, would provide all of the vegetable oil India now imports. In addition, more than twice as much seed meal and more than 25 million tonnes of livestock fodder would be supplied. The value of the forage would be slightly greater than the value of the oil and the seed meal combined.

Egypt imports a half-million tonnes annually of vegetable oil. Only 3 percent of its land is under cultivation, and most of that is in the Nile Delta and along the thousand-kilometer length of the great river as it courses through the Egyptian desert--a thin green ribbon of agriculture. Yet, Egypt borders on the Mediterranean, the Red Sea, and the Gulf of Aqaba. These coastlines total 2,140 kilometers, or more than twice the length of the Egyptian Nile.

If Egypt's coastal areas inland for 4 kilometers were planted with SOS-7 and irrigated with seawater, the area (856,000 hectares) would be larger than the entire Nile Valley. The halophyte crop would yield a half-million tonnes of vegetable oil, eliminating the need for imports. The crop would also supply a million tonnes of seed meal (or twice as much as is now imported) and 11.4 million tonnes of fodder-- sufficient to meet 80 percent of the forage requirements of all of Egypt's buffalo, cattle, sheep, goats, and camels.

The crop would save Egypt about a quarter of a billion dollars annually in hard-currency imports. What is more significant is that by switching over oilseed and forage production to seawater-irrigated halophytes, Egypt would free up those freshwater-irrigated croplands that are now producing alfalfa--the equivalent of 700,000 hectares. These fertile lands could then be used to produce grain or vegetable crops such as rice, wheat, or tomatoes.

Similar projections may be made for other arid, tropical regions meeting primary physical and economic criteria: a seacoast, a shortage of fresh water, a warm climate, a market need for oilseed or forage crops, and the prospect of financial support from internal or international agencies. North African, Middle Eastern, and Eastern nations are most appropriate, although there are coastal deserts in Latin America as well.

It is by now self-evident what impact these developments could have on water resources and on those various international relationships traditionally affected by water resource allocation. There are obvious temptations to extrapolate beyond that.

For example, an emotionless perspective might suggest that improved water resources might be another thread by which to begin the task of untangling that most complex of Gordian Knots--the riddles and passions of the Middle East. To the sophisticate, this would seem hopelessly naive.

116

There are no emotionless perspectives in the Middle East. And traditionally, such knots are untied by a far different instrument.

Temptations to extrapolate further should be resisted by all but the boldest political scientists--but then, one might consider that...

7

Turkey's Peace Pipeline

Cem Duna

In February 1987, during his state visit to the United States, Prime Minister Turgut Ozal first introduced the idea of building two water piplines from Turkey to other parts of the Middle East. The "Peace Pipeline" project would allow Turkey to share water from the Seyhan and Ceyhan rivers with other countries in the region.

Both rivers originate and flow entirely in Turkey. They follow parallel courses on a north/south axis and empty into the Mediterranean Sea at the Bay of Iskenderun. The average daily flow of the rivers is a total of 39.17 million cubic meters (MCM), of which Turkey plans to utilize approximately 23.07 MCM for irrigation or hydroelectric power generation. The remaining 16.1 MCM passes into the Mediterranean.

Intent on utilizing this unused flow, the government of Turkey engaged the services of Brown & Root International, Inc., to conduct technical and economic prefeasibility studies for the water pipeline project.

The Western Pipeline would pump 3.5 MCM of water per day through a pipeline covering a distance of approximately 2,700 kilometers. The pipeline would vary in size from between 3 and 4 meters in diameter. Pumping stations would be built along the route to lift water over high terrain, and power stations would also be built to generate the required electricity. The Western Pipeline would consist of two phases, the first stretching to Amman and supplying water to the cities of Aleppo, Hama, Homs, Damascus. The

second phase would parallel the first and lead to
the Saudi Arabian cities of Tabuk, Medina, Yanbu,
Mecca, and Jeddah. The cost for the Western
Pipeline is estimated at $8.5 billion. It is
expected to provide 8 to 9 million people with up
to 400 liters of water per person per day. Water
could be distributed to the various cities in the
quantities indicated in Table 7.1.

The Gulf Pipeline could include the cities of
al-Kuwait (Kuwait); ad-Dammam, al-Khubar, and al-
Hofuf (Saudi Arabia); al-Manamah (Bahrain); Doha
(Qatar); and Abu Dhabi, Dubai, Sharjah, Ras al-
Khaimah, Fujairah, Ajman and Umm Al Qaiwaing
(United Arab Emirates) and Muscat (Oman). The
total pipeline length is approximately 3,900
kilometers, through which 2.5 MCM would be pumped
per day. An estimated 6 to 7 million people could
be served with up to 400 liters per day by this
pipeline, which estimates indicate would cost
$12.5 billion. The daily distribution of water
that could be made from the pipeline is shown in
Table 7.2. Because of topographical factors, the
Gulf Pipeline would require fewer pumping stations
than the Western Pipeline, which in turn means
lower power, operation, and maintenance costs.

Both pipelines could be built in eight to ten
years. Hence, they should be regarded as long-
term projects only. The individual countries must
develop their own strategies for the short-term.
It is anticipated that the major portion of each
pipeline would be built from prestressed concrete
cylinder pipe that could be manufactured in the
region. Construction costs would thus be reduced.
The figures for the cost of each pipeline--$8.5
billion and $12.5 billion--include overall
construction, operations and maintenance, and
electrical generation costs.

Water transported by both pipelines will be
of fairly high quality and will require limited
treatment, mainly chlorination. This water is
intended primarily for domestic consumption.
Although seasonal demand may vary, the flow in the
pipelines will tend to remain constant into
receiving reservoirs. Also, both pipelines are
expected to supplement existing supplies and not
compete with them. For example, water from the
pipelines is not intended to replace that produced
by desalination.

120

The cost of the project will not be prohibitive, especially when compared with other processes such as desalination. The average cost of water delivered for the Western Pipeline and Gulf Pipeline has been calculated at $0.84 per cubic meter and $1.07 per cubic meter, respectively, which compares favorably to the subsidized cost of water from desalination plants. Hence, the water from both pipelines could prove to be a cost-effective supplement to other sources in the region.

Financing for the project could likely be secured from a variety of sources. International organizations such as the International Bank for Reconstruction and Development (IBRD) and the Islamic Development Bank could be part of a larger consortium that would also include investment banks and other private institutions. Contributions from user nations would also be used in any financing plan. In addition, the countries using water from the pipeline would be responsible for the maintenance of those sections of the pipelines within their respective territories.

Technically, financially, and ecologically, the project is a feasible one. The only real obstacle is political. The interests that need to be reconciled are so polarized that one can easily claim that the creation of a common denominator is not possible. What is needed is to convince each user country—many of whom are age-old adversaries—that it is in their long-term interests to build, operate, and protect this lifeline and not to create yet another hostage to the controversies of the region. The government of Turkey is now calling on other countries to join in this effort. Turkey is committed to bringing together all parties in a spirit of cooperation and community.

Although the Turkish government recognizes the obstacles standing in the way of this cooperation, it believes that common sense will prevail. As Prime Minister Turgut Ozal has stated, by increasing economic collaboration and pooling regional resources, the political tension in the area can be diffused. Ultimately, this cooperation can lead to a common prosperity, the preservation of which would be in the joint interest of these nations. In other words, increased economic contacts will be the catalyst for the building of a common future for the region. This, in turn, would lead to a greater role for the Middle East in the global community.

It is for this reason, therefore, that the government of Turkey, has named this project the "Peace Pipeline." It believes that human beings, when supplied with a basic necessity such as water, would rather preserve this resource than deprive their adversaries and, ultimately, themselves and their loved ones. It will be on the foundation of this understanding that peace may be built, inch by inch, but solid enough to secure a future to which we may all look with confidence.

TABLE 7.1
Distribution for Western Pipeline

Location	Cubic Meters/Day
TURKEY	300,000
SYRIA	
Aleppo	300,000
Hama	100,000
Homs	100,000
Damascus	600,000
JORDAN	
Amman	600,000
SAUDI ARABIA	
Tabuk	100,000
Medina	300,000
Yanbu	100,000
Mecca	500,000
Jeddah	500,000
Total	3,500,000

Source: Brown & Root International, Inc.,
Prefeasibility Studies.

Table 7.2
Distribution for Gulf Pipeline

Location	Cubic Meters/Day
KUWAIT	600,000
SAUDI ARABIA	
Jubail	200,000
ad-Dammam	200,000
al-Khubar	200,000
al-Hofuf	200,000
BAHRAIN	
al-Manamah	200,000
QATAR	
Doha	100,000
UAE	
Abu Dhabi	280,000
Dubai	160,000
Sharjah/Ajman	120,000
Ras al-Khaimah/Fujairah/	
Umm al Qaiwan	40,000
OMAN	
Muscat	200,000
Total	2,500,000

Source: Brown & Root International, Inc.,
Prefeasibility Studies.

8

U.S. Government Policy Structure

Joyce R. Starr and Daniel C. Stoll

In a speech in 1987 before leading U.S. water experts, M. Peter McPherson, then administrator of the United States Agency for International Development, noted that the "development...of water resources is a critical foreign policy issue" for the United States.[1] Since the 1950s, the U.S. government, through a variety of departments and agencies, has undertaken extensive technical assistance programs and development projects in the Middle East. Projects for every conceivable purpose have been designed and implemented including wastewater treatment plants, feasibility studies for dams, and training programs for regional experts.

In this chapter we present an assessment of federal agencies working on water resources development in the Middle East. We emphasize areas of agency responsibility, programs, agency interaction, and constraints on development efforts. This analysis focuses on the role of the federal agencies in tracking emerging water problems, in gathering data and information, and in creating development programs. Also included is a description of bilateral commissions and foundations that are involved with Middle East water projects.

UNITED STATES DEPARTMENT OF STATE

The Department of State has a long and successful involvement with regional water issues.

Among the offices tracking these questions is the Bureau for Near Eastern and South Asian Affairs (NEA). Within NEA, country desk officers and the Office for Regional Affairs monitor developments in the region. Embassy staffs (especially in Amman and Tel Aviv) closely follow water issues. In general, the NEA's work addresses the political, rather than economic, dimension of the water problems and rarely involves overarching water policy concerns. With little opportunity for long-term, in-depth studies, both embassy and NEA analysts offer near-term assessments of fast-breaking events and, then, only if developments are directly linked to U.S. interests.

The Bureau of Oceans and International Environmental and Scientific Affairs (OES) coordinates the U.S. government's participation in international environmental activities. It also works closely with USAID, the U.S. Environmental Protection Agency (EPA), and other agencies in monitoring environmental trends around the world. The State Department's Bureau of Intelligence and Research likewise studies water problems within the region on a high-priority basis, especially those related to international boundary issues.

The State Department takes the lead in all diplomatic efforts on water disputes; the renowned Johnston Plan of the early 1950s exemplifies its capabilities and commitment. Unfortunately, proposed budgetary and staff cuts could reduce the department's effectiveness in coordinating long-range diplomacy, planning, and analysis.

In 1987, the department announced that, because of budget cuts, the activities of various bureaus may have to be consolidated. Continued reduction in funding and the regrouping that will result could weaken the State Department's stature and effectiveness in international water-dispute resolution.

United States Agency for International Development

Responsibility for water resources development in foreign countries rests primarily with the United States Agency for International Development (USAID). Serving as the U.S.

government's principal funding agency for development efforts, USAID has experience in all facets of water resources management: water pollution control, water conservation and reuse, management master planning, hydropower studies and facilities, irrigated agriculture, and wastewater treatment.

The agency has undertaken feasibility studies for the politically sensitive Maqarin Dam on the Yarmuk River, funded the rehabilitation of hydroelectrical equipment for Egypt's Aswan High Dam, and conducted master planning studies for domestic water supply, wastewater treatment, and irrigation projects in Egypt, Jordan, and Syria. In 1987 the agency had begun implementing programs for major water and wastewater facilities in Egypt and Jordan. The wide range of USAID water projects are shown in Table 8.1.

USAID-sponsored programs typically have been implemented by U.S. private-sector firms working jointly with host country architectual, engineering, and construction firms. USAID's current portfolio of active or planned water-related projects in the Middle East is extensive: Over $2.5 billion has been spent or allocated for fiscal years (FY) 1975-1986.

The USAID Bureau for Asia and the Near East is responsible for the coordination of policy and technical components of Middle East water projects. The Office of Project Development, Office of Technical Resources, and the desks for specific countries are involved in this process. The Bureau for Science and Technology oversees the work of the Water for Sanitation and Health Project (WASH).

Until 1986, there was a USAID Water Resources Committee within the Bureau for Asia and the Near East. This working group acted as a formal information center and coordinating body for water experts within the bureau. Although the committee lacked policymaking authority, its members did explore policy options and emerging issues. Because of changes in the emphasis and scope of USAID's water resources development program, however, the committee was disbanded.

USAID has extensive involvement in large-scale infrastructure projects in the Middle East and Pakistan. These include capital-intensive programs in water supply, sewerage, and irrigation. Although USAID is still committed to completing projects in these areas (for example, Cairo's wastewater system), there is an increased emphasis on funding complementary activities, which focus on operations and maintenance, technical assistance, and training. USAID is also involved in the review of selected industrial pollution control issues.

There are two reasons for this shift in emphasis. First, because several Near East countries already have highly developed water infrastructures, the maintenance of existing facilities has become a priority. One example is Jordan, whose water infrastructure is so advanced that USAID has turned its attention to the fine tuning of Jordan's management approach.

Second, even when expansion in the infrastructure is required, USAID has been forced to move away from expensive construction projects because of a lack of funding. Cutbacks imposed by the Gramm-Rudman-Hollings legislation limit USAID's ability to support infrastructure growth; a number of major capital projects in Egypt are still under way.

USAID often uses the prospect of future funding to influence structural reform. In concert with appropriate foreign government agencies, for example, USAID missions establish benchmarks for equitable user charges and water rates. The objective is to ensure that water utilities and facilities achieve greater cost recovery and eventually become financially self-supporting. Policy dialogue with Near East governments can also encourage improved operation and maintenance procedures, as well as proper training and adequate compensation for the staff personnel who operate water facilities. USAID strives to affect both short-range improvements and long-range reforms.

UNITED STATES DEPARTMENT OF THE INTERIOR

United States Geological Survey

Since 1945, the United States Geological Survey (USGS), through its Water Resources Division's Office of International Hydrology, has undertaken no less than ninety-five water programs in the Near East, funded primarily by USAID and governments in the Gulf. These include scientific and technical exchanges, workshops, and technical assistance programs. Table 8.2 presents a list of USGS projects from 1964 to 1986. In addition, the USGS has made a concerted attempt to train and educate foreign technicians in advanced water technologies. In 1986, however, the Office of International Hydrology was phased out, and all international water resources activities undertaken by the USGS are now handled through the Office of the Assistant Chief Hydrologist for Research and External Coordination.

The USGS is not an international policymaking body and does not maintain missions in foreign countries. It can, however, participate in projects at the invitation of a host government, another U.S. agency, or a multinational funding organization. The USGS has worked extensively with the U.S.-Saudi Arabian Joint Commission on Economic Cooperation, for example. With commission funds, the USGS cooperatively prepared a water atlas containing data on all aspects of Saudi Arabian water resources. This atlas could serve as a basis for long-range Saudi projections and planning. With commission backing, the USGS also created a training program for Saudi hydrological technicians; in the past ten years over 400 technicians have graduated from this program.

The USGS cooperates with USAID in conducting surveys, data collection, and analyses on groundwater and surface water resources. For example, the USGS has provided extensive assistance to the Natural Resources Authority of Jordan and the Jordan Valley Authority.

The 1984 Water Resources Research Act designated the USGS as coordinator for water

resources research institutes in the United
States. The act also called for the creation of a
desalination research program, which has not yet
been funded but could maintain a strong
international emphasis.

Bureau of Reclamation

Chartered in 1902 to develop irrigation
projects in seventeen states in the western United
States, the bureau's activities have been
broadened to include work in foreign countries.
Like the USGS, the bureau's Division of Foreign
Activities provides technical assistance only at
the invitation of other U.S. agencies,
multilateral funding organizations, or host
governments. In cooperation with USAID, the
bureau is currently advising the Egyptian
Electricity Authority on the replacement of
turbines and runners for the Aswan High Dam and
and is advising the Egyptian Ministry of
Irrigation on the installation of an automated
hydrologic data collection system in the Nile
River basin. The bureau also conducted a review
of all water development projects in Sudan and
prepared an update of the Nile Waters Study.
Among other issues, this review addressed the
feasibility of rehabilitating and modernizing the
Gezira irrigation project and of reducing
sedimentation resulting from the Roseries Dam.
The department's recent decision to
restructure the Bureau of Reclamation will
undoubtedly affect activities outside the western
United States. Both staff reductions and the
shift in emphasis from construction projects to
water quality and conservation activities will
require the redefinition of the scope of the
Bureau of Reclamation's international role.

UNITED STATES DEPARTMENT OF AGRICULTURE

The U.S. Department of Agriculture (USDA) has
three organizations that provide support for its
international activities. Those groups concerned
with water resources are the Office of

International Cooperation and Development (OICD), the Soil Conservation Service, and the Agriculture Research Service.

Office of International Cooperation and Development

The international activities of the USDA are coordinated by the Office of International Cooperation and Development. The principal source of its funding is USAID, although monies are also provided by the World Bank, the United Nations Food and Agriculture Organization (FAO), and host countries.

One of the most successful programs in the Middle East is the Trinational Agriculture Technology Exchange and Cooperation (TATEC) Research Project, staffed by Egyptian, Israeli, and U.S. scientists. Formed in July 1984, with a $2.5-million grant from USAID's Near East Regional Cooperation Program, the project encourages cooperation among Egyptian, Israeli, and U.S. scientists in promoting agricultural innovations in Egypt and Israel. To date, research undertaken has focused on the intensification of farm system production, medicinal use of desert flora, and disease, pest, and weed control.

Soil Conservation Service

The Soil Conservation Service (SCS) worked in cooperation with the USGS on the Saudi Water Atlas. SCS engineers are currently conducting irrigation studies in Egypt and long-term geohydrology studies for Jordan. The SCS has also provided personnel to support a review of range management in Jordan and its impact on water resources management.

Agricultural Research Service

Drawing from USAID Public Law 480 funds, the Agricultural Research Service (ARS) supervises several research projects in the Middle East,

including cooperative research between regional
and U.S. scientists. ARS also participates in the
administration of the joint U.S.-Israel Binational
Agricultural Research and Development Fund (BARD),
which seeks advances in the areas of irrigation,
dryland agriculture, salt-tolerant crops, and
advanced agricultural technologies. ARS is
presently active in irrigation water management
projects in Egypt and in dryland agricultural
systems research in Jordan.

UNITED STATES DEPARTMENT OF DEFENSE

The Department of Defense closely tracks
water issues as they relate to U.S. military
interests in the Middle East. The Water Resources
Management Action Group (WARMAG), for example,
plans for the provision of potable water to troops
in the field, eliminating water as a wartime
constraint.

Defense Intelligence Agency

The Defense Intelligence Agency (DIA) also
monitors regional resource trends. Specifically,
the DIA focuses on three areas: scarcity of water
as grounds for potential conflict; implications
of water scarcity for economic development and
political stability; and implications of water
supply for large-scale military operations in arid
environments.
The last major nonclassified study
commissioned by the DIA on Near East water
resources was in 1983. The Office of the Deputy
Assistant Secretary for Near Eastern and South
Asian Affairs currently maintains no ongoing
research capability on water resources.

United States Army Corps of Engineers

The reputation of the Army Corps of Engineers
dates back to the founding of West Point in 1802,
when the academy's graduates formed the core of
engineering expertise in the United States.

Today, the Army Corps of Engineers is involved in all aspects of construction and engineering relating to water resource development, including: flood control, hydropower, supply conservation, potomology (the study of rivers), and coastal protection.

The corps serves as a planning and advisory body, responding to requests from both U.S. and foreign governments. According to Lieutenant General E. R. Heiberg III, chief of the Army Corps of Engineers, "our recommendations are based on what we call the three 'Es': engineering feasibility, economic sense and, increasingly, ...environmental sensitivity."[2] General Heiberg estimates that 30 percent of all corps engineering dollars and over two-thirds of its employees (approximately 14,000 people) are engaged in water resource work. Although the corps relies on in-house capabilities for technology and feasibility studies, the majority of its construction projects are actually executed by private companies, both domestic and foreign. Of a total budget of $10 billion, it is estimated that $8-9 billion is dispensed in payments to individual contractors.

Perhaps the best example of the "macro" approach used by the Army Corps of Engineers may be seen in the assistance given to the nine African countries of the Niger River Basin Authority. This project, executed in conjunction with USAID, resulted in the compilation of all available data pertinent to the basin's development. A central computer is able to analyze hypothetical situations or desired changes, such as erecting a hydropower plant at a certain location, and projects the ramifications of such decisions. The project thus supplies crucial information for effective decision making where there is enormous competition over limited water resources.

A recent achievement for the corps is the Three Gorges Dam Project on the Upper Yangtze River in China. The dam may well have a potential power generation of up to 13,000 megawatts. The Army Corps of Engineers also provided technical assistance to India for a project involving the reduction of pollution in the Ganges River and serves in an advisory capacity for the Panama Canal Commission.

UNITED STATES ENVIRONMENTAL PROTECTION AGENCY

Working through its Office of International Activities, the U.S. Environmental Protection Agency is currently supporting a number of water-related research projects in Egypt using P.L. 480 funds. These include industrial pollution research, water quality studies of the Nile River, and research into the environmental effects of pesticides.

FOUNDATIONS AND COMMISSIONS

The U.S. government foundations and commissions listed below could serve as prototypes for expanded U.S.-foreign cooperation on water development projects.

U.S.-Saudi Arabian Joint Commission on Economic Cooperation

Established in 1974 to "promote cooperation...in the fields of industrialization, trade, manpower training, agriculture, and science and technology,"[3] the Joint Commission is a bilateral organization that relies on Saudi development funds. U.S. authorities provide technical counsel and expertise. To date, approximately $1.25 billion has been spent on commission-sponsored activities. With the Treasury Department as U.S. coordinator, the commission has enlisted the services of virtually every agency of the U.S. government, including the Departments of Agriculture, Commerce, Energy, Health and Human Services, Interior, Labor, and Transportation.

Calling on the expertise of the United States Geological Survey, the commission initiated and prepared the Saudi Water Atlas. The commission also established the Agriculture and Water Project, which publishes an updated series of water resource reports and funds basic research in soil and water management. It has worked with the Saudi Saline Water Conversion Corporation (the largest organization of this type in the world) and has sponsored research and development work related to harnessing the region's abundant solar energy for desalination.

Although the commission has contributed considerably to building Saudi Arabia's water infrastructure, momentum has been lost in the mid-1980s. The decline in oil prices has reduced support for water resource programming. Moreover, with both Saudi Arabia and the United States increasingly preoccupied with other pressing regional concerns, the commission is receiving less attention from both governments. Nonetheless, it remains an important model for international cooperation on water resources.

U.S.-Israel Binational Agricultural Research and Development Fund

BARD was established in 1977 to encourage cooperative agricultural research and development efforts by Israel and the United States. Administrative decision making and management are shared through equal representation on a board of directors and a technical advisory committee.

The fund accepts short-term proposals (two to three years in duration) from institutions of higher learning, government agencies, and nonprofit organizations. Since 1977, approximately $63 million has been awarded for 374 different research projects. Among those projects have been efforts focused on water resource management, methods of increasing agricultural yields, development of new plant types with high drought resistancy, and soil management.

BARD has been instrumental in the development and installation of computerized monitors, which check soil conditions for moisture levels, thereby reducing unnecessary irrigation. Research on the relationship between soil and water has been conducted, including a study of soil composition and its effect on the absorption and retention of water. Experiments have also been undertaken on the use of reprocessed water for irrigation.

U.S.-Israel Binational Science Foundation

Established in 1972 to promote cooperation between the United States and Israel on scientific research efforts, the Binational Science Foundation (BSF) awards grant monies for research in the health, life, and social sciences and in physics, chemistry, and mathematics. At present, spending by the foundation averages $7.5 million per annum.

SUMMARY

The U.S. government has a strong history of involvement in Middle East water resources development. By investing substantial sums of money and committing the combined expertise of its various bureaus and departments, the federal government has emerged as a powerful force in shaping development trends in the region. Overall, its wide-ranging activities have contributed substantially to regional economic growth, improvements in the standard of living, and better health conditions.

At the same time, the U.S. government's efforts could be enhanced by instituting reforms in three areas:

*   Long-range planning
*   Coordination among U.S. agencies dealing with water resources
*   Addressing increased staffing requirements

Despite well-intentioned efforts, federal departments and agencies working with water issues seldom undertake comprehensive, anticipatory planning on critical problems. Time, budgetary, and personnel constraints preclude a macro approach when dealing with regional conditions. Also, the sheer number of issues requiring attention is beyond the scope of any single agency. Government experts are well aware of the crucial questions that should be answered but are forced to respond on an ad hoc basis.

An emphasis on long-term planning and improved

coordination is essential. A new interagency committee should be established to formulate and realize long-range planning goals. The creation of a centralized data base on water projects would reduce duplication of effort and increase the sharing of information and expertise.

Finally, staff continuity within each agency should be encouraged to provide greater consistency in project design and execution. At present, fairly rapid staff turnover means that projects planned by one group of experts are often completed by another. Assignments of longer duration would ensure greater coherency and strengthen "institutional memory."

NOTES

1. M. Peter McPherson, administrator, United States Agency for International Development (Presentation at U.S. Foreign Policy on Water Resources in the Middle East and Horn of Africa Conference, Center for Strategic and International Studies, Washington, D.C., 20 February 1987).

2. E. R. Heiberg, chief of engineers, U.S. Department of the Army (Presentation at U.S. Foreign Policy on Water Resources in the Middle East and Horn of Africa Conference, Center for Strategic and International Studies, Washington, D.C., 21 February 1987).

3. Annual report, 1984-1985, of the United States-Saudi Arabian Joint Commission on Economic Cooperation.

TABLE 8.1
U.S. Agency for International Development Capital
and Technical Assistance Projects Involving Water
Resource Issues in the Middle East
(FY 1975-1987)

Country	Project Name	Planned Life of Project Funding Level $ Millions
Egypt	Water Use and Management	13.0
	Canal Maintenance	25.0
	Cairo Water Supply	91.0
	Irrigation Pumping	8.0
	Canal Cities Water and Sewerage (Phase I)	169.0
	Housing and Community Upgrading	60.0
	Alexandria Sewerage	213.7
	Cairo Sewerage	
	Phase I: Rehabilitation	129.0
	Phase II: New Construction	816.0
	Industrial Pollution Control Subproject	27.0
	Mineral, Petroleum, and Groundwater Project	7.0
	Irrigation Systems Management	139.5
	Science and Technology for Development	3.0
	Rehabilitation and Modernization of Aswan High Dam	100.0
	Decentralization Program (water, wastewater, drainage)	400.0
	Water and Wastewater Institutional Development	15.0
	Sinai Planning Studies	1.0
	Irrigation Pumping	8.0
	Subtotal	2,225.2

138

Jordan	Maqarin Dam Feasibility Study	1.0
	Jordan Valley Irrigation	
	Design/Maqarin Dam	14.0
	Sprinkler Irrigation Equipment	4.5
	Rift Valley Water Resources	5.0
	Maqarin Dam and Jordan Valley	
	Irrigation System	9.0
	Water Management Technology	1.3
	Aqaba Wastewater	7.5
	Amman Water/Sewerage	39.0
	Irbid Water/Sewerage	53.5
	Zarqa Ruseifa Water/	
	Wastewater	15.0
	Groundwater Resources	
	Investigation	5.0
	Water Systems and Services	
	Management	21.0
	Groundwater Assessment	4.0
	Technical Services and	
	Feasibility Studies Project	5.0
	Subtotal	**184.8**
Lebanon	Potable Water I	6.5
	Potable Water and	
	Environmental Sanitation	7.7
	Emergency Water Repair	4.0
	Subtotal	**18.2**
Israel	Joint U.S./Israel	
	Desalination Project	20.0
	Subtotal	**20.0**
West Bank/ Gaza Strip	Various water, wastewater, and stormwater management activities	5.0
	Subtotal	**5.0**
Syria[a]	Damascus Water Supply II	14.5
	Euphrates Basin Irrigation	7.1

Provincial Water Supply	17.6
Damascus Water Supply I	48.0
Subtotal	87.2
Total	2,540.4

[a]Program discontinued by the U.S. government in late 1983.
Source: Information compiled by authors from 1975-1987 USAID presentations to Congress.

Table 8.2

United States Geological Survey Projects in the
Middle East 1964-1986

Country	Project	Sponsor
Jordan	Installation of geophysical well logging tapes on Jordan's computer	USAID
Jordan	Assistance in hydrologic data bank installation	USAID
Jordan	Groundwater evaluation project in Jordan	USAID
Saudi Arabia	Assistance in the storage and retrieval of hydrologic data SAS computer system	Govt. of Saudi Arabia
Saudi Arabia	Water Atlas: monitoring quality control and final printing	Govt. of Saudi Arabia
Saudi Arabia	Assistance in developing step-backwater rating curves	Govt. of Saudi Arabia
Saudi Arabia	Assistance in final printing of Water Atlas, quality control	Govt. of Saudi Arabia
Qatar	Assistance in artificial recharge of Qatar's main aquifer	Govt. of Qatar
Saudi Arabia	Assistance in final printing of Water Atlas	Govt. of Saudi Arabia

Saudi rabia	Project review and collection of information for statistical report	Govt. of Saudi Arabia
Jordan	Assistance in organic analysis and data interpretation	USAID
Turkey	Evaluation of project on Karstic water resources research	UNDP and USGS
Saudi Arabia	Assistance in installation of meteorological equipment, instruction in its use, and establishment of maintenance and calibration procedures	Govt. of Saudi Arabia
Saudi Arabia, Jordan, United Arab Emirates (UAE)	Project review and formulation	Govt. of Saudi Arabia and USAID
Jordan	Calibrate flow model, North Jordan Ground Water Project	USAID
United Arab Emirates (UAE) and Kuwait	Prepare reconnaissance assessment of water resources and advise on artificial recharge (Kuwait)	Govts. of UAE and Kuwait

Source: Information compiled from authors'
interview with Marshall Moss, assistant chief
hydrologist, United States Geological Survey, 13
August 1986 in Washington, D.C.

9

Water for the Year 2000

Joyce R. Starr and Daniel C. Stoll

By the year 2000, water--not oil--will be the dominant resource issue of the Middle East. According to Worldwatch Institute, "despite modern technology and feats of engineering, a secure water future for much of the world remains elusive."[1] The prognosis for Egypt, Jordan, Israel, the West Bank, Gaza Strip, Syria, and Iraq is especially alarming. If present consumption patterns continue, emerging water shortages, combined with a deterioration in water quality, will lead to more desperate competition and conflict.[2]

The following is an abridged version of the final report issued from our year-long research project, "U.S. Foreign Policy on Water Resources in the Middle East." It provides an overview of conditions within the Middle East and recommendations for policy changes.

THE JORDAN RIVER BASIN

With headwaters originating in the Syrian and Lebanese highlands, the Jordan River has an average annual discharge of 1,287 million cubic meters (MCM). Its principal tributary, the Yarmuk, forms the border between Syria and Jordan and divides Israel from Jordan in the Yarmuk Triangle. The Jordan River itself demarcates the boundary between Israel and Jordan.

Conditions will be severe in the Jordan River basin. By the year 2000, Israel's water needs may exceed supply by 30 percent, with Jordan experiencing a 20 percent discrepancy.[3] The upper Jordan River already has been developed to maximum capacity. If construction of the proposed Unity/Maqarin Dam proceeds, the Yarmuk--the only major undeveloped tributary--will also become fully utilized. Moreover, the quality of surface and groundwater supplies is deteriorating at a rapid pace, thereby requiring substantial investment in domestic and industrial wastewater treatment, groundwater recharge programs, and water quality monitoring. Some experts now predict that Jordan and Israel will have fully developed all renewable sources of water by 1995 and will reach a critical point in the exploitation of nonrenewable water supplies unless remedial measures are taken quickly.

Quiescent rivalries may well be rekindled and sharpened as Syria continues implementation of development schemes for the upper Yarmuk. These plans could lead to increased salinity levels in the lower Yarmuk and lower Jordan rivers, lower water levels in the Dead Sea, and reduced irrigation water for Jordan's East Ghor Development Project. From a strategic point of view, this long-term Syrian effort could reduce Jordanian access to the Yarmuk, which Jordan relies on for irrigation in the Jordan Valley, and may affect downstream availabilities for Israel.[4] Ultimately, the possibility of heightened tension or even armed conflict among the riparians could increase dramatically.

Israel

Israel transfers water from the Jordan basin via the National Water Carrier to western portions of the country. Israel is already using 95 percent (of an estimated total of 1,755 MCM per annum) of its renewable resources and consumes five times more water per capita than do its neighbors. Current total consumption for Israel is estimated at 1,750 MCM per annum.[5]

Although Israel has managed to reduce the amount of water used in agriculture by 15 percent over the last two years, this reduction has not

144

appreciably eased the strain on existing sources.[6] If estimates are correct, by the year 2000 Israel will face shortages up to 800 MCM per annum--almost half of its present consumption. Because approximately 75 percent of the water Israel currently consumes is used for agriculture, substantial future reductions in water use by the agricultural sector could avert the crisis.[7] Given the dominant role agricultural interests have on Israel's politics and economy, however, such hard choices are viewed as unlikely.

Jordan

Thomas Naff of the University of Pennsylvania estimates that in 1985, total consumption in Jordan was approximately 870 MCM. He also predicts that annual demand could reach 1,000 MCM per annum by the year 2000, resulting in an annual water deficit of 170 to 200 MCM.[8] Jordan uses approximately 130 MCM of water a year from the Yarmuk River for irrigated agriculture in the Jordan basin.

In 1987 Jordan and Syria ratified an agreement allowing for construction of the Unity Dam at the Maqarin site. The 100 meter-high dam is expected to have a storage capacity of 220 MCM per annum and will help regulate the flow of the Yarmuk, expand irrigated agriculture in the Jordan valley, and provide water for municipal and industrial use in upland Jordan. This agreement also limits the scope of Syrian development plans in the Yarmuk basin.

Syria

Syria's development program for the Yarmuk basin calls for building a series of medium and small dams that eventually could divert up to 40 percent of the Yarmuk's waters--if the terms of the agreement with Jordan are not observed.[9] Without a Jordanian agreement, a complete Syrian plan would take a decade and would sharpen rivalries over decreasing quantities of water.

For Jordan, Syrian diversion of the Yarmuk could mean the loss of significant amounts of water. Jordan is expending most of its share of the Yarmuk waters for agriculture in the Jordan Valley. In addition, Yarmuk water is also pumped through pipelines to upland urban centers such as Irbid and Amman for municipal and industrial purposes.

The West Bank and Gaza Strip

According to the West Bank Data Project's The West Bank handbook, "The main water potential of the West Bank, shared with Israel, is exploited to its limit, in a ratio of 4.5 percent to the West Bank and 95.5 percent to Israel."[10] The handbook also notes that water authorities plan to allocate 137 MCM per year to the West Bank Arab population (approximately 1 million people) by the decade's end and 100 MCM for the Jewish population (100,000 people). Yet, in 1985 Jewish settlements in the region already exceeded their water quotas by almost one-third.[11]

The water situation in the Gaza Strip has been described as a "time bomb waiting to explode."[12] Indeed, the large Gaza Strip aquifer, which supplies all of the area's water needs, is already seriously overpumped. In 1985, annual agricultural and domestic consumption outstripped natural replenishment of the aquifer by almost 50 percent.[13] This overpumping has resulted in partial contamination of the aquifer by seawater intrusion.

Contamination of water supplies in the Gaza Strip is reaching critical proportions. The heavy use of pesticides and fertilizers in the Gaza Strip also presents a potential source of groundwater pollution. Raw sewage in many towns is still not being collected or treated. A 1987 Israeli state comptroller report on the West Bank and Gaza Strip's civil administration noted that sewage in these areas could devastate underground aquifers. The report warned that "if a solution is not expedited...the problem will cause greater damage, and the financial investment required will be much greater than it would be today."[14] New sewage systems in the Gaza Strip alone would cost in excess of $16 million at 1988 prices.[15] Israel has refrained from making significant investments in West Bank and Gaza Strip water and wastewater services over the last decade. United Nations organizations, bilateral donors, USAID, and nongovernmental organizations have attempted to address this need but only in a piecemeal fashion.

TIGRIS/EUPHRATES RIVER BASINS

Both the Tigris and Euphrates rivers originate in the mountains of eastern Turkey. The Euphrates flows through Syria and Iraq to the head of the Gulf, whereas the Tigris flows directly through Iraq, obtaining additional flows from major tributaries rising in the Zagros Mountains of Iran and discharging in the Gulf. The combined drainage basin of the two river basins is approximately 1,118,260 square kilometers. The approximate annual discharge of the Tigris is 42,230 MCM and 31,830 MCM for the Euphrates.

Decreasing water quantities and deteriorating water quality will be dominant points of controversy in the Syrian, Iraqi, and Turkish triangle in the near future.

Turkey

Ambitious development schemes in Turkey, especially the Southeast Anatolia Project (GAP), are reducing the discharge of the Euphrates, which directly affects both Syria and Iraq. Development projects in all three countries are seriously eroding the quality of both surface and groundwater supplies, truncating domestic and agricultural use. Some relief may be found in Turkey's recent proposal to share its abundant resources from the Ceyhan and Seyhan rivers with other Middle East nations via a "Peace Pipeline," although some experts still question this project's political and economic viability.

Syria

Conditions in Syria are difficult to assess. Neither U.S. government agencies such as USAID nor multilateral organizations such as the World Bank are currently undertaking development projects in Syria. Data related to Syrian water projects are tightly controlled by the government, but experts believe the country could face a general deficit as high as 1 billion cubic meters (BCM) by the year 2000 if present patterns of consumption continue.[16] Syria is confronting mounting shortages, the result of reduced flow from the Euphrates and from contamination by pesticides, fertilizers, and salt. Even now, major cities like Damascus and Aleppo suffer from constant water and electricity shortages (from hydroelectric sources), especially during the summer months. Proposed large-scale agricultural projects, if poorly designed and constructed, will only further damage the quality of existing water supplies.

Alarmed by these conditions, the Syrian government has sharply increased the amounts budgeted for water and hydroelectric projects in 1988. Figures released by Damascus indicate these areas will account for 43.5 percent of the government's investment budget in 1988, compared with only 10 percent in prior budget cycles.[17] Targeted projects include badly needed water and sewage systems in Damascus, Aleppo, Homs, and Hama.

Iraq

As a consequence of its ongoing war with Iran, Iraq has slowed the pace of development efforts and even suspended several major projects. Iraq is also concerned about Turkey's massive Southeast Anatolia Project--a program of 13 hydroelectric and irrigation projects on the upper Tigris and Euphrates rivers. Despite Turkey's assurances, some experts estimate that the GAP could reduce the annual Euphrates flow into Iraq from 30 BCM to 11 BCM once it is completed. Iraq estimates its minimum requirement for Euphrates

148

water is approximately 13 BCM.[18] Syrian
development efforts are also causing alarm in
Iraq. Iraq claimed that almost 3 million Iraqi
farmers were adversely affected when Syria reduced
the flow of the Euphrates to fill the reservoir
behind the Ath-Thawrah Dam in 1975. Indeed, the
dam brought these two countries to the brink of
war. Moreover, as the final riparian along both
the Tigris and Euphrates rivers, Iraq is most
harmed by increased pollution from upstream
development. Conditions have deteriorated so
markedly in some areas that villages are now
forced to import drinking water by truck.[19]

THE NILE RIVER BASIN

The longest river in the world, the Nile and
its headwaters flow through nine African states:
Sudan, Ethiopia, Egypt, Uganda, Tanzania, Kenya,
Zaire, Rwanda, and Burundi. The Nile basin covers
approximately one-tenth of the African continent.
The average annual discharge of the Nile is
approximately 84,000 MCM.

Drought in the Horn of Africa and unusually
low rainfall during the early 1980s focused world
attention on the Nile River basin, particularly on
Ethiopia and Sudan. Although rainfall briefly
returned to a more normal level and improved the
situation somewhat, countries sharing the basin
still confront the specter of periodic drought,
deteriorating water quality, and, in some areas,
starvation. History has shown that cooperation on
resource management and development among the nine
riparians of the Nile has been difficult to
achieve. In 1983, however, a consultative body
known as the Undugu Group was formed to promote
cooperation on wide-ranging issues. This group
could prove to be a forerunner for more extensive
resource coordination.[20]

Egypt

Egypt is almost totally dependent on the
waters of the Nile. As a result, extractions
upstream reduce the availability of water for

149

Egypt's ever-expanding internal demands and impair electricity generation from the Aswan Dam. Egypt has long recognized the importance of monitoring the development schemes of upper riparians but has almost no influence in actual planning or execution.

Reliable data on Egyptian water use is sparse, and seasonal flows of the Nile are difficult to calculate. The government of Egypt, with support from the World Bank, has undertaken comprehensive studies on the country's resources, but much of this information remains restricted. Statistics relating to anticipated demand and future availability of supplies are subject to qualification. The work of John Waterbury, however, presents one of the most exhaustive and authoritative collations to date. Waterbury projects total Egyptian demand for water at 73 BCM by 1990, at present rates of water efficiencies.[21] Because of the ongoing drought in the Nile Basin, water availability for Egypt in 1988 is projected to fall between 49,000 MCM and 55,500 MCM--the worst and best case scenarios, respectively.[22] Presently, water shortfalls exist. The drought notwithstanding, by the turn of the century, Egypt could experience a critical water shortfall, particularly against the backdrop of seemingly unstoppable population growth. Increased pollution, especially in the delta and in selected coastal areas, will exacerbate this reality.

CAUSES AND RAMIFICATIONS

These water crises may be traced to three primary causes: increased water consumption, which is linked to population growth, expansion of industry and agriculture, and increased urbanization; inefficient maintainance and improper operation of water facilities; and poor cooperation among countries sharing common resources.

Startling statistics on population growth in the countries under study have been provided by the Population Reference Bureau, as shown in Table 9.1. To help understand the magnitude of the problem confronting countries in the region, the average annual discharge rates of the river basins in question are detailed in Table 9.2. In examining Table 9.1, keep in mind that a natural annual population increase of 1 percent or lower is generally considered "manageable." The United States and other Western nations have rates equal to or well below the 1 percent level. Rates of 1.5 percent and above can have catastrophic consequences for developing nations. In this regard, the countries under study are caught in a population spiral spinning out of control. As domestic, agricultural, and industrial demands mount, many countries will confront extreme difficulty in providing sufficient quantities of water to their citizens. Even Israel, with its comparatively modest growth rate of 1.6 percent per annum, will be forced to wrestle with the consequences of a seriously overextended resource infrastructure.

Poorly managed and inefficient water facilities--dams, water and wastewater treatment plants, industrial facilities, and irrigation schemes--have emerged as another priority. Although USAID, World Bank, and other international agencies have worked assiduously to create water infrastructures throughout the Middle East, most of these facilities now operate well below peak efficiency levels. In Egypt and Syria, in particular, technicians and engineers employed in water treatment and sewage plants typically lack the skills and expertise required to operate sophisticated machinery and monitor complicated processes. All countries examined here suffer from inadequately maintained and poorly operated infrastructure facilities.

Budgetary constraints also prohibit governments from adequately maintaining water infrastructures once they are completed and commissioned. Even when money is available for maintenance or training programs, governments are often reluctant to tackle the problem, preferring to channel funds to the construction of additional facilities. During the past twenty years, the majority of Middle East water projects have been cofinanced with multilateral and bilateral foreign assistance, chiefly to improve water quality and public health conditions in primary and secondary urban areas. Hence, governments commonly assume that future efforts will be financed in a similar manner.

Finally, there is little or no collaboration among countries sharing common resources. Almost all major water resources in the region (surface and groundwater alike) are shared by two or more states. Maximum utilization of all supplies necessitates far-reaching cooperation. In a region beset by ethnic, religious, and political hostility, however, neighborly goodwill has seldom been achieved in the past and may become even more elusive in the future.

Syria, Turkey, and Iraq have had difficulty in collaborating on the use of the Euphrates River. This was observed most recently when Turkey announced its Southeast Anatolia Project, which was designed without comprehensive Syrian and Iraqi consultation. The Trilateral Commission on the Euphrates River, whose members are Turkey, Syria, and Iraq, has only discussed technical matters such as river flow and rainfall data. Further, because Turkey regards the area of the Tigris and Euphrates rivers as one basin and Iraq views the rivers and their basins as separate entities, the difference could prove to be an obstacle in finalizing any future water agreement. Despite the fact that the GAP will affect the flow into Syria and Iraq and is thus of immediate concern to both, Turkey has so far rejected suggestions for high level negotiations on water allocation and use. Instead, Turkey has agreed only to the creation of a low-level technical exchange commission. As a result, the World Bank has been reluctant to provide funding for project components until a cooperative water-sharing agreement is secured.

Similarly, Syria, Israel, and Jordan have never formally agreed on use of the Jordan River. The most far-reaching plan for basinwide development was proposed in the early 1950s by Eric Johnston, President Eisenhower's special ambassador to the Middle East. Although technical understandings were reached and Israel and Jordan still tacitly operate under many of the plan's provisions, political intransigence and distrust derailed formal acceptance of the Johnston Plan.[23]

The proposed Unity/Maqarin Dam, of primary importance to Jordan, has yet to be built. Situated along the Yarmuk between Syria and Jordan, the dam would contribute substantially to more efficient utilization of the river. In short, it would help regulate the flow of the Yarmuk by creating a storage facility and would thereby prevent scarce water from being wasted by minimizing water discharge to the Dead Sea. Jordan and Syria ratified an agreement to proceed with building a smaller facility--the Unity Dam-- at the Maqarin site in 1987. Some experts doubt whether this project will materialize, however, because of the need for a riparian agreement with Israel prior to construction of the dam.

Water resources will undoubtedly affect the outcome of negotiations on the Palestinian question. Recent reports of Israeli intentions to pump more water from the West Bank's aquifers elicited sharp protests from West Bank Arabs and from Jordan. With available renewable resources in Jordan, Israel, and the West Bank approaching their limits in development, the area will not be able to sustain a major influx of new users.

Along the Nile, with nine riparians sharing the same sources of water, relations are even more convoluted. Although attempts to establish a legal regime for the river date back to the late nineteenth century, there is still no single agreement binding all the states. The United Nations Development Program (UNDP) workshop for Nile basin countries in Bangkok, in January 1986, took preliminary steps toward achieving a larger, more detailed formula, but substantially more work must be undertaken to bring this formula to fruition. The workshop participants also agreed to seek the assistance of the UNDP in creating a Nile development program. The Undugu Group could become a forum for such future cooperative efforts.

Ethiopia remains the "great unknown" of the Nile basin and will assume a more dominant role in the 1990s. Waterbury estimates that Ethiopia is the source of more than 82 percent of the Nile's water. Given this preeminent position, development plans undertaken by Ethiopia--such as irrigation schemes in the Blue Nile basin and the

Baro--could have a deleterious impact on Egypt and Sudan.

Finally, the region's water resource quagmire is even deeper than technical, management, or economic constraints would suggest. More difficult to assess and alter are underlying passions. Although actual physical conditions vary from nation to nation, attitudes about water do not: In every country, access to clean water is considered an undeniable right, and tampering with water supplies is considered an unspeakable crime. Especially in more traditional agricultural areas, consumption patterns reflect deeply ingrained, age-old feelings about water. Water determines the nature of economic survival, permeates cultural norms, and infuses political ideology. Although technology may be harnessed, emotions pose the ultimate challenge.

A NEW ROLE FOR THE U.S. GOVERNMENT?

How can the U.S. government effectively respond to these emerging problems? U.S. government and private sector representatives participating in our year-long research project agreed that the United States can and should remain deeply involved in water development efforts in the Middle East. Toward this end, it is recommended that the government concentrate on four policy areas:

* Development of advanced water technologies

* Encouragement of more efficient
  resources management and
  conservation strategies

* Improvement in coordination among U.S.
  agencies dealing with water issues

* Attention to long-range research and
  planning

These goals could be met through the specific structural and programmatic changes described in the next section. These measures can be taken at

minimal cost, with high returns. Small, practical
investments today would preclude the need for
massive aid in the future. Congressional
awareness of the looming Middle East water
resources crisis and support for a strengthened
U.S. government position is essential.

POLICY EMPHASES

Emphasize Development of Advanced Water
Technologies. Although technology is not a panacea
for the region's problems, experts participating
in this project argued that technology can reduce
the strain on existing water supplies. Advanced
technologies could prove invaluable in several
respects.

Desalination of salt water and brackish water
could supplement current supplies. Granted, the
capital investment and energy expenses now
associated with desalination make it prohibitive
for many Middle Eastern countries. Still,
improvements in the process--especially those
related to reduced energy costs--would heighten
its attractiveness in the future.

Attention should also be given to protecting
and extending existing resources. Advanced water
reuse technologies, for example, would recycle
precious supplies. Although recycled water is
already employed in agriculture, future efforts
could concentrate on selected domestic and
industrial uses. Overall, these methods must be
made more cost-effective and reliable under local
conditions.

Improved pollution control and water
treatment processes will also help safeguard water
quality. Contamination of surface and groundwater
supplies from agricultural, municipal, and
industrial sources is a growing problem in many
Middle East countries. Procedures must be
developed both to treat already contaminated water
and to neutralize pollutants before they damage
supplies. Special emphasis should be given to
utilizing the region's abundant solar energy in
wastewater treatment processes.

Advanced agricultural technologies should
also be encouraged. Drip or center-pivot

irrigation systems regulate the application of water to crops and thus reduce waste and loss through evaporation. Plant breeding and high value crops maximize the economic benefits of limited water supplies.

The U.S. government has been exploring ways to encourage technological advances through bilateral commissions and foundations. These initiatives could be strengthened to include a wider range of technical applications: reducing costs for desalination processes, applying solar energy to water technologies, improving horticulture and aquaculture, and others.

It should be recognized that advanced technologies are not appropriate or necessarily better in all situations; sophisticated processes such as drip irrigation cannot be employed effectively without well-trained technicians to operate and maintain the systems. Technology can serve a vital function, but only if applied judiciously and with sensitivity to social, political, and economic conditions.

<u>Encourage Foreign Governments to Adopt More Efficient Resources Management and Conservation Strategies</u>. Experts from the Middle East and U.S. government alike point out that the region's water problems stem as much from improperly used resources as from increased demand. To varying degrees, the countries we have examined suffer from poorly maintained utilities, improperly designed water projects, and inadequately trained staffs for water facilities. These three conditions are interrelated, and each compounds the effects of the others, thereby exacerbating the strain placed on scarce supplies.

Particularly urgent is the inadequacy of personnel operating and maintaining water infrastructures. Lack of incentive to keep standards high, low salary levels, and an absence of encouragement for professional responsibility all contribute to continuing personnel difficulties. In addition, physical problems in water systems add to infrastructure difficulties. For example, enormous amounts of water are lost in urban areas through leaks in distribution systems and contamination by untreated or partially treated sewage. Many industrial facilities use water-intensive technologies that are inappropriate for the region.

Poor initial planning on project designs impose even greater burdens. This is most apparent in the case of large-scale irrigation schemes. In Iraq, improperly planned and executed irrigation projects have led to the abandonment of large tracts of land in the lower Mesopotamian plain. In Egypt, faulty drainage systems have saturated agricultural land, resulting in a higher water table, increased salinity, and numerous health problems.

The United States should accelerate training programs to familiarize specialists from the region in advanced water management and conservation techniques. Expanded training programs would also encourage regional self-sufficiency. USAID, the Bureau of Reclamation, the USGS, and other agencies have extensive experience in training personnel from Egypt, Jordan, Saudi Arabia, Sudan, and other nations. The U.S. government should build upon existing programs, rather than undertake major new initiatives.

Improve Coordination Among U.S. Agencies Involved with Water Development Issues. There is a need to improve coordination and communication among U.S. government agencies concerned with water issues. This is a result in part of the wide variety of activities undertaken and the sheer number of organizations involved. Experts within the U.S. government acknowledge their inability to follow the work of counterparts in other agencies--primarily a reflection of inadequate staff levels. Only the Department of State and USAID have a joint committee on Near East water resources issues that meets regularly.

Hence, a centralized process for policy coordination, program planning, and data collection should be established for Middle East water projects. Experts could then easily draw upon past efforts, while keeping their counterparts throughout the government informed of ongoing work or anticipated programs.

Encourage Long-Term Research and Planning to
Identify Emerging Issues and to Offer Possible
Policy Responses. The U.S. government has
traditionally lacked the means or capability to
undertake long-term studies on water resource
trends in the international arena. Even when a
specific division within a major agency does track
evolving water issues, the focus is rarely
anticipatory. Budgetary and personnel constraints
result in a reactive approach, rather than
anticipation or prevention of a crisis certain to
emerge.

A process through which long-term assessments
can be conducted and future policy initiatives
outlined is sorely needed. Analyses of the
viability of proposed major programs, like the
Turkish Peace Pipeline or the Maqarin/Unity Dam in
Jordan, should be undertaken.

It should be noted that anticipatory planning
is conducted on famine and drought. As a response
to the 1984-1985 crisis in Ethiopia, the
interagency Famine Early Warning System (FEWS) was
created. Based in the Office of Technical
Resources within USAID's Bureau for Africa, FEWS
uses information supplied by the National
Aeronautics and Space Administration (NASA), USGS,
National Oceanic and Atmospheric Administration
(NOAA), and other sources to track a variety of
conditions in eight African countries to determine
the likelihood of another African drought.

RECOMMENDATIONS FOR CHANGE

Based on these policy needs, we recommend
that the United States government undertake the
following:

Creation of a Coordinating Body Within the
U.S. Government. A central coordinating body
should be established within the U.S. government
for all Middle East water research and development
programs. This interagency group would serve as a
data clearinghouse and "institutional memory" for
the government's work on water issues.

It should be the responsibility of this
interagency coordinating body to alert the U.S.

government to potential water crises. This body would not detract from or diminish the responsibility of agencies already working on water problems: the Department of State would continue to formulate overall policy with the input of USAID, and the USGS and Bureau of Reclamation would continue their technical assistance outreach. The proposed body would, however, bring greater continuity to U.S. government efforts. Its primary function would be to track problems rather than initiate new programs and, therefore, would reinforce existing policy.

The executive branch should designate an agency within the U.S. government to serve as the secretariat for this coordinating body. An annual report, drawing on both unclassified and classified data, would be presented to the Congress and executive branch each year.

Create a U.S.-Middle East Water Program to Encourage the Development of Advanced Water Technologies. This multilateral program could be loosely patterned after existing bilateral commissions and foundations. Topics of study would cover a wide range of technical issues, including: pollution control, horticulture, water-reuse strategies, and the application of solar energy to water technologies. Special emphasis on research related to desert regions would have applications for both the Middle East and the U.S. Southwest. The program would also undertake research in the social sciences pertinent to the human dimension of water issues.

For greatest effectiveness, this program should come under the auspices of the U.S. interagency coordinating body we have proposed. The secretariat of this body would also serve as the secretariat for the multilateral Middle East water program. The program would be apolitical. Regional experts would be engaged, both as representatives of their respective governments and as water authorities in their own right. A consortium of U.S. academic and private-sector research institutions should be engaged in this process. Research would be shared with all participating countries. The program would in no way be linked to the Arab-Israeli peace process.

Although the majority of the program's initial funding would derive from the U.S. Congress, participating nations would also be asked to contribute. Many experts felt that start-up funding should be within the $5-10-million range over a period of three years to give the program an adequate base from which to begin its important task.

NOTES

1. Sandra Postel, Conserving Water: The Untapped Alternative, Worldwatch Report #67 (Washington, D.C.: Worldwatch Institute, 1985), p. 5.

2. Consumption patterns in most countries are often a function of pricing policies. Most experts both in the United States and the countries examined here believe that present water subsidies will not be reduced dramatically in the years ahead for internal political reasons. Hence, impending shortages will be exacerbated.

3. Thomas Naff and Ruth Matson, eds., Water in the Middle East: Conflict or Cooperation? (Boulder, Colo: Westview Press, 1984), p. 229.

4. Ze'ev Schiff, military correspondent, Ha'aretz; interview with Joyce R. Starr, Tel Aviv, Israel, 21 August 1987.

5. Joe Stork, "Water and Israel's Occupation Strategy," MERIP Reports 13, no. 116 (1983):19.

6. Meir Ben-Meir, director general of Israel's Ministry of Agriculture; interview with Joyce R. Starr, Tel Aviv, Israel, 15 August 1987.

7. Stork, "Water and Israel's Occupation Strategy, " p. 20.

8. Thomas Naff, "Water: An Emerging Issue in the Middle East?" The Annals of the American Academy of Political Scientists, November 1985, p. 68.

9. Interview with Ze'ev Schiff.

10. Meron Benvenisti, The West Bank Handbook: A Political Lexicon (Boulder, Colo: Westview Press, 1986), p. 223.

11. Elaine Ruth Fletcher, "Territories' Water Supply Drying up with Overuse," Jerusalem Post, 2 July 1987, p. 4.

12. Interview with Ze'ev Schiff.

13. Fletcher, "Territories' Water Supply Drying up with Overuse," p. 4.

14. Ibid.

15. Ibid.

16. Off-the-record interviews with World Bank officials, September 1986.

17. "Syria's Budget: Where the Cash Flows in '87," The Middle East (May 1987): 33.

18. Ewan Anderson, "The Current Water Crisis in the Middle East" (Paper presented at the U.S. Foreign Policy on Water Resources in the Middle East and Horn of Africa Conference, Center for Strategic and International Studies, Washington, D.C., 20 February 1986), p. 23.

19. Abdul-Amir al-Anbari, ambassador of Iraq; interview with Joyce R. Starr, 2 November 1987, Washington, D.C.

20. Mohammed el-Diwany, minister, Embassy of Egypt (Remarks at The Nile River Basin: A Case Study in Riparian Relations Conference, Center for Strategic and International Studies, Washington, D.C.), 4 February 1987.

21. John Waterbury, Hydropolitics of the Nile Valley (Syracuse, N.Y.: Syracuse University Press, 1979, p. 226.

22. Robert O. Collins, professor of history, University of California at Santa Barbara and Michel Pommier, division chief, Country Department III - Infrastructure Europe, Middle East & North Africa Region, The World Bank; interviews with Joyce R. Starr, Washington, D.C., 15 March 1988.

23. Selig Taubenblatt, international business consultant (Presentation at U.S. Foreign Policy on Water Resources in the Middle East: Instrument for Peace and Development Conference, Center for Strategic and International Studies, Washington, D.C., 25 November 1986).

TABLE 9.1
Population Growth in the Middle East

	Population mid-1986 (millions)	Crude Birth Rate (per 1,000 pop.)	Natural Increase (annual, %) (millions)	Population Projected to Year 2000
Egypt	50.5	37	2.6	71.2
Sudan	22.9	46	2.9	34.2
Iraq	16.0	46	3.3	24.2
Israel	4.2	23	1.6	5.3
Jordon	3.7	44	3.7	6.4
Lebanon	2.7	29	2.1	3.6
Syria	10.5	47	3.8	17.2
Turkey	52.4	35	2.5	69.7
U.S.	241	16	0.7	268
World	4942	27	1.7	6157

Source: World Population Data Sheet (Washington, D.C.:
The Population Reference Bureau, Inc., 1986).

TABLE 9.2
Average Annual Discharge Rates

Jordan River[a]	1,287 MCM
Euphrates River	31,820 MCM
Tigris River	42,230 MCM
Nile River	84,000 MCM

Source: Compiled by authors from U.S. government sources.
[a]Statistic taken from the Johnston Plan (1956).

Bibliography

BOOKS AND PERIODICALS

Abu-Zeid, Mahmoud A. "Irrigation and Drainage Projects Preparation," Water Management for Arid Lands in Developing Countries, Asit Biswas et al., eds. (Oxford: Pergamon Press, 1980), pp. 111-118.

Accession de l'Ouganda a l'Accord portant création de l'organization pour l'aménagement et le développement du bassin de la rivière Kagera. Bujumbura, Le 19 Mai 1981. United Nations, Natural Resources Water Series No. 13, Treaties Concerning the Utilization of International Water Courses for Other Purposes than Navigation, Africa, (New York, 1984).

Adburgham, Roland, "Potential for Much Greater Output," Financial Times, 19 May 1986, p. 6.

Ahmad, Z. H. "Solar Earth-Water Stills," Solar Energy, 20 (1978): 387-391.

Allan, J. A. "Irrigated Agriculture in the Middle East: The Future," Agriculture Development in the Middle East, Peter Beaumont and Keith McLachlan, eds. (New York: John Wiley and Sons, 1985).

Amir, Ilan, and Benjamin Zur. "Irrigation in Arid Zones: The Israeli Case," Arid Zone Settlement, Gideon Golany, ed. (New York: Pergamon Press, 1979), pp. 411-439.

Amiran, David H. K. "Geographical Aspects of National Planning in Israel: The Management of Limited Resources," Institute of British

<u>Geographers</u> 3, no. 1 (1978): 115-128.

Anderson, Ewan. "The Current Water Crisis in the Middle East." Paper presented at the Center for Strategic and International Studies Conference on U.S. Foreign Policy on Water Resources in the Middle East and Horn of Africa, Washington, D.C., 20 February 1986.

"Ataturk Dam: A Tale of High Intrigue," <u>Middle East Economic Digest</u> Special Report (November 1983): 26-33.

Baddour, A. I. <u>Sudanese-Egyptian Relations: A Chronological and Analytical Study</u> (The Hague: M. Nighoff, 1960).

Badr, G. M. "The Nile Waters Question: Background and Recent Development," #15 <u>Egyptian Review of International Law</u>, (1979).

Barchard, David. "Turkey Hits Trouble over Middle East Exports," <u>Financial Times</u>, 2 September 1986, p. 4.

_____. "Iraq Signs Contract for 1 Billion Pound Dam Plant," <u>Financial Times</u>, 30 September 1986, p. 6.

Bari, Zohwal. "Syrian-Iraqi Dispute Over the Euphrates Waters," <u>International Studies</u> (New Delhi) 16, no. 2 (April-June 1977): 227-244.

Barre, Finn. "Saudis to Subsidize Barley," <u>Financial Times</u>, 24 September 1986, p. 40.

Bartholet, Jefferey. "Mediterranean's Pearl Now Awash in Sewage," <u>Washington Post</u>, 21 August 1986, p. 29.

Beaumont, Peter, and Keith McLachlan, eds. <u>Agricultural Development in the Middle East</u> (New York: John Wiley and Sons, 1985).

Beaumont, Peter, Blake Gerald, and Malcolm Wagstaff, eds. <u>The Middle East: A Geographical Study</u> (New York: John Wiley and Sons, 1976).

Benedick, Richard Elliot. "The High Dam and the Transformation of the Nile," <u>Middle East Journal</u> 33, no. 2 (Spring 1979): 119-144.

Ben-Shahar, Haim, et al. <u>The Research Project for Economic Cooperation in the Middle East: An Overview</u> (Tel Aviv: Tel Aviv University, 1986).

Benvenisti, Meron. <u>1986 Report: West Bank Data Project</u> (Boulder, Colo.: Westview Press, 1986).

166

_____. _The West Bank Handbook: A Political Lexicon_ (Boulder, Colo.: Westview Press, 1986).

Bodgener, J. "Oman Develops Skills Ancient and Modern," _The Middle East Economic Digest_, 10 August 1984, p. 38.

"Brief," _Middle East Economic Digest_ 28, no. 33 (17 August 1984): 7.

"Brief," _Middle East Economic Digest_ 28, no. 39, (28 September 1984): 18.

Brilliant, Joshua. "Water in the Hills," _Jerusalem Post Magazine_, 4 May 1979, p. 14.

Brown, Lester, ed. _State of the World, 1987_ (New York: W. W. Norton & Company, 1987).

Butter, David. "Egypt: Edging Toward Economic Reform," _Middle East Economic Digest_ 28, no. 32 (10 August 1984): 10-13.

_____. "Prospects Brighten for Egypt's Cotton Harvest," _Middle East Economic Digest_ 28, no. 33 (17 August 1984): 6.

Caelleigh, Addeane. "Middle East Water: Vital Resource, Conflict, and Cooperation," _A Shared Destiny: Near East Regional Development and Cooperation_, Joyce R. Starr, ed. (New York: Praeger, 1983), pp. 121-136.

Cassell, Michael. "Urban Water Supplies and Sewage: Current Development Projects," _Middle East Annual Review_ (New York: R a n d McNally, 1979).

Charnock, Anne. "Bold Steps Taken to Boost City Supplies," _Middle East Economic Digest_ 28, no. 32 (10 August 1984): 29-30.

_____. "Nile Schemes Bring Benefits and Problems," _Middle East Economic Digest_ 28, no. 32 (10 August 1984): 30.

_____. "Turkey, Iraq Harness Rivers' Power," _Middle East Economic Digest_ 28, no. 32 (10 August 1984): 35-36.

_____. "Water Resources: Strategic Concerns Speed Search for New Answers," _Middle East Economic Digest_ 28, no. 32 (10 August 1984): 27-28.

Cooley, John. "Syria Links Pullout to Guaranteed Access to Water," _Washington Post_, 8 June 1983.

_____. "The War over Water," _Foreign Policy_, no. 54 (Spring 1984): 3-26.

Cooper, J., and A. Nozik. "Hydrogen Production Using Photocatalytic Semiconductor Powers and Colloids" (Golden, Colo.: Solar Energy Research Institute unpublished report, 1985).

Crusoe, Jonathan. "Bouygues Plays Key Role in Iraqi Barrage Effort," Middle East Economic Digest 28, no. 32 (10 August 1984): 35.

Davis, Uri, E. I. Antonia, and John Richardson. "Israel's Water Policies," Journal of Palestine Studies 9, no. 2 (Winter 1980): 10-11.

Delyannis, A., and E. Delyannis. "Solar Distillation Plants of High Capacity," Fourth International Symposium on Fresh Water from the Sea, Vol. 4 (1973): 487-491.

Derrick, Jonathan. "Is the Middle East Drying Up?" The Middle East (no. 157 (October 1987): 28.)

Deudney, Daniel. Rivers of Energy: The Hydropower Potential, Worldwatch Papers, no. 44 (Washington, D.C.: Worldwatch Institute, 1981).

Drysdale, A., and A. G. Blake. The Middle East and North Africa: A Political Geography (Oxford: Oxford University Press, 1985).

"Egypt: Threat to Nile Water," African Recorder 19 (14 July 1980): 5 and 396.

El-Diwany, Mohammed. Remarks at a seminar entitled "The Nile River Basin: A Case Study in Riparian Relations," Center for Strategic and International Studies, Washington, D.C., 4 February 1987.

El-Gabaly, M. M. "Problems of Soils and Salinity," Water Management for Arid Lands in Developing Countries, Asit Biswas et al., eds. (Oxford: Pergamon Press, 1980).

"Euphrates Dam Gives Syria Headaches," An-Nahar Arab Report, 19 March 1984, pp. 20-21.

"Euphrates Dam Transforms Neglected Areas," Middle East Economic Digest, special report (March 1980), pp. 33-35.

Fahim, Jussein M. D. People and Environment: The Aswan High Dam Case (New York: Pergamon Press, 1981).

Fletcher, D. B. "UV/Ozone Process Treats Toxics," Waterworld News, May/June 1987, pp. 25-28.

Fletcher, Elaine Ruth. "Territories Water Supply

Drying Up With Overuse," Jerusalem Post, 2 July 1987.

Galnoor, Itzhak. "Water Policymaking in Israel," Policy Analysis, 4 (1978): 339-365.

Garg, S. K., et al. "Development of Humidification-Dehumidification Techniques for Water Desalination in Arid Zones of India." Paper presented at the 2nd European Symposium on Fresh Water from the Sea, Athens, May 9-12, 1967.

Garretson, Albert H. and R. D. Hayton. "The Nile Basin." The Law of International Drainage Basins, (New York: Oceana Publications, Inc., 1967).

_____. "The Nile River System." Proceedings of the American Society of International Law at its Fifty-Fourth Annual Meeting held at Washington, D.C., April 28-30, 1960, (1960).

George, Alan. "Wrangle Over the Euphrates," The Middle East (no. 157 (October 1987): 27.)

Godana, Bonaya Adhi. Africa's Shared Water Resources: Legal and Institutional Aspects of the Nile, Niger and Senegal River Systems (London: Frances Pinter, 1985).

Goshko, John. "Cut Things Not People," Washington Post, 29 October 1979, p. A23.

Gowers, Andrew. "Bridging Egypt's Food Gap," Financial Times, 13 February 1987, p. 30.

Graham, J. L., and R. Dellinger, "A Laboratory Evaluation of the Solar Incinerability of Hazardous Organic Wastes," SERI Progress Report (Dayton, Ohio: University of Dayton, 1985).

Graham-Brown, Sarah, and Richard Barchard. "Turkey Taps the Euphrates Resources," Middle East Economic Digest 25, no. 29 (17 July 1981): 50-52.

Groundwater in the Eastern Mediterranean and Western Asia, Natural Resources/Water Series, no. 9 (New York: United Nations, 1982).

Guariso, G. "A Real-Time Management Model for the Aswan High Dam with Policy Implications," Geographical Analysis 13, no. 4 (October 1981): 355-371.

_____. "Nile Water for Sinai: Framework for Analysis," Water Resources Research 17, no. 6 (December 1981): 1585-1593.

Guariso, G., et al. "Energy, Agriculture, and Water: A Multiobjective Programming Analysis of the Operations of the Aswan High Dam," Environment and Planning, 12 (1980): 369-379.

Gustafson, C. Don. "The Irrigation Problem: The Israeli Experience," Israel, the Middle East, and U.S. Interests, H. Allen and I. Volgys, eds. (New York: Praeger, 1983), 55-56.

Harding, J. "Apparatus for Solar Distillation," Proceedings of the Institute of Civil Engineers, 72 (1983): 284-288.

"Health Standards Rise Sharply," Middle East Economic Digest 28, no. 36 (7 September 1984): 12.

Heiberg, Lieutenant. General E. R. Speech given at the Conference at the Center for Strategic and International Studies on U.S. Foreign Policy on Water Resources in the Middle East and Horn of Africa, Washington, D.C., 21 February 1987.

Hewett, R. "Preliminary Assessment of the Feasibility of Utilizing Solar Thermal Technology to Detoxify Pink Water," SERI, 1986.

Hodges, C. N., et al. "Solar Distillation Using Multiple-Effect Humidification" Unpublished report prepared for the Office of Saline Water Research Development Progress 194, U.S. Department of the Interior, 1966.

Hosni, Sayed. "The Nile Regime." Egyptian Review of International Law #17.

Hsaio, C. C., C. Le, and D. F. Ollis. "Heterogeneous Photocatalysis: Degradation of Dilute Solutions of Dichloromethane (CH_2Cl_2), Chloroform ($CHCl_3$), and Carbon Tetrachloride (CCl_4) with Illuminated TiO_2 Photocatalyst," Journal of Catalysis, Volume 82, no. 2 (Academic Press, 1983).

Inbar, Moshe, and J. O. Maos, "Water Resource Management in the Northern Jordan Valley," KIDMA 7, no. 3 (1983): 21-25.

"Iraq Sides with Turkey Against Syria on Use of Euphrates Resources," Middle East Times, 12 May 1984.

"Iraqi Water Treatment Plant Project," Financial Times, 21 January 1986, p. 28.

"Iraqi Water Treatment Projects," <u>Financial Times</u>, 23 April 1986, p. 27.

"Israel Bought a Third of South," <u>Arab Report and Record</u>, 1-15 January 1978, p. 12.

Ivekovic, H. "Water by Dehumidification of Air Saturated with Vapor Below 80° C," <u>Fifth International Symposium on Fresh Water from the Sea</u>, vol. 2 (1976): 456-457.

Jabber, Paul. "Egypt's Crisis: America's Dilemma," <u>Foreign Affairs</u> (Summer 1986): 960-980.

Jenkins, Loren. "Dynamic Mayor Remakes Istanbul," <u>Washington Post</u>, 24 September 1986, p. 14.

Kassas, M. "An Environmental Science Programme for an International River Basin: A Case Study," <u>Water Management for Arid Lands in Developing Countries</u> (Oxford: Pergamon Press, 1980).

Kats, Gregory. "To the High Dam with CARE," <u>Cairo Today</u>, October 1983, pp. 27-31.

Keen, M. "Cheaper, Purer Water from the Sun," <u>Water and Sewage</u>, 5 August 1985, pp. S14-S16.

Khouri, Rami. "Dead Sea Swan Song," <u>The Middle East</u>, (no. 70 (August 1980): 44.)

_____. "Jordan's Ten Billion Dollar Hothouse," <u>The Middle East</u>, (no. 71 (September 1980): 76.)

Land, Thomas. "Flushing the Desert," <u>The Middle East</u>, (no. 153 (July 1987): 39).

Latif, M. G. "Solar Desalination" M.Sc. thesis, El Minia University, Egypt, 1983.

Lawand, T. A. "Systems for Solar Distillation," Paper presented at the International Conference for Appropriate Technologies for Semi Arid Areas: Wind and Solar Energy for Water Supply, West-Berlin, 15-20 September 1975.

Lusk, Gill. "Sudan Budget: What Do the Figures Mean?" <u>Middle East Economic Digest</u> 28, no. 37 (14 September 1984): 37.

Lycett, Andrew. "Special Survey: Water Resources," <u>The Middle East</u>, (no. 84 (October 1981): 79-82.)

Mazur, Michael P. <u>Economic Growth and Development in Jordan</u> (London: Croom Helm, 1979).

McConnel, Pat. "Ataturk Dam: The Biggest Yet," <u>The Middle East</u>, (no. 115 (May 1984): 52, 75-76.)

McPherson, M. Peter. Paper presented at the Center for Strategic and International

Studies Conference on U.S. Foreign Policy on Water Resources in the Middle East and Horn of Africa, Washington, D.C., 20-21 February 1986.

Midwest Research Institute, SOLERAS (Kansas City, Mo.: 1986).

Mohsen, Assem Abdul. "Egypt, Ethiopia Clash over Nile," The Middle East, (no. 71 (September 1980): 70.)

Montagnon, Peter. "Turkey Wins Generous Terms on $233M Loan," Financial Times, 22 January 1986, p. 30.

Moustofa, S. M., D. I. Jarrar, and H. I. El-Mansy. "Performance of a Self-Regulating Solar Multistage Flash Desalination System," Solar Energy 35, no. 4 (1985): 333-340.

Naff, Thomas and F. W. Frey. "Water: An Emerging Issue in the Middle East?" Annals of the American Academy of Political Science, no. 482 (November 1985): 65-84.

Naff, Thomas, and Ruth Matson eds. Water in the Middle East: Conflict or Cooperation (Boulder, Colo: Westview Press, 1984).

Noor-Abboud, Abed, and Jonathan Crusoe. "Iraq: Saline Waste Goes Down the Drain," Middle East Economic Digest 28, no. 33 (17 August 1984): 10.

Odone, Toby. "Manmade River Brings Water to the People," Middle East Economic Digest, 10 August 1984, pp. 39-40.

Okidi, C. O. "Legal and Policy Regime of Lake Victoria and Nile Basins." Indian Journal of International Law #20, (1980).

Ollis, D. F. Heterogeneous Photocatalysis for Water Purification:Prospects and Problems (Raleigh: North Carolina University, 1984).

Osborn, D. E. Spectrally Selective Beam Splitters Designed to Decouple Quantum and Thermal Solar Energy Conversion in Hybrid Concentrating Systems (Tucson: University of Arizona, 1987).

Ottaway, David. "Water Issue Roils Turk-Syrian Ties," Washington Post, 19 May 1984.

Perera, J. "Water Geopolitics," The Middle East, February 1981, pp. 47-54.

Postel, Sandra. Water: Rethinking Management in an Age of Scarcity, Worldwatch Paper, no. 62

(Washington, D.C.: Worldwatch Institute, December 1984).

_____. Conserving Water: The Untapped Alternative, Worldwatch Paper, no. 67 (Washington, D.C.: Worldwatch Institute, September 1985).

Prengle, H. W., C. E. Mauk, and J. E. Payne. "Ozone/UV Oxidation of Chlorinated Compounds in Water." Paper presented at the International Ozone Institute Forum on Ozone Disinfection, Chicago, Ilinois, 2-4 June 1976.

Pruden, A. L., and D. F. Ollis. "Photoassisted Heterogeneous Catalysis. Degradation of Trichloroethylene in Water." Journal of Catalysis (vol. 82, no. 2, Academic Press, 1983).

Roberts, John. "Pakdemirli Unveils Turkish Investment Plans," Middle East Economic Digest 28, no. 39 (28 September 1984): 34.

Rogers, Peter. "Water: Not As Cheap As You Think," Technology Review 139, no. 8 (November/December 1986): 30-43.

Royal Scientific Society. West Bank Resources and Its Significance to Israel, April 1979, pp. 7-10.

Saliba, Samir N. The Jordan River Dispute (The Hague: Martinus Nijhoff, 1965).

Samaha, M., and M. Abu-Zeid. "Strategy for Irrigation Development in Egypt up to the Year 2000," Water Supply and Management, vol. 4 (Oxford: Pergamon Press, 1980), pp. 139-146.

Samman, Nabil. "Cost-Benefit Analysis of the Euphrates Dam," Water Supply and Management 5, no. 4/5 (1981): 331-338.

Schmida, Leslie Keys to Control-Israel's Pursuit of Arab Water Resources (Washington, D.C.: American Educational Trust, 1982).

Selwyn, Michael. "Ethiopia's Ten-Year Plan Is in with a Chance." Middle East Economic Digest 28, no. 38 (21 September 1984): 10.

Simpson, Barbara, and I. Carmi. "The Hydrology of the Jordan Tributaries: Hydrographic and Isotopic Investigation," Journal of

Hydrology, 62 (1983): 225-242.

Sinai, Anne, and Allen Pollack, eds. Hashemite Kingdom of Jordan and the West Bank (New York: American Academic Association for Peace in the Middle East, 1977), pp. 65-113.

Solar Thermal Power, SERI/SP-273-3047 (Golden, Colo.: Solar Energy Research Institute, 1987).

Spector, Lea, and George E. Gruen. Waters of Controversy: Implications for the Arab-Israel Peace Process. (New York: American Jewish Committee, Institute of Human Relations, December 1980), pp. 1-11.

Starr, Joyce R., ed. A Shared Destiny: Near East Regional Development and Cooperation. (New York: Praeger Publishers, 1983).

Stauffer, Thomas. "Israel's Water Needs May Erode Path to Peace in Region," Christian Science Monitor, 20 January 1982, pp. 78-79.

_____. "The Lure of the Litani," Middle East International, 30 July 1982, pp. 13-14.

Stork, Joe. "Water and Israel's Occupation Strategy," MERIP Reports 13, no. 116 (1983): 227-283.

"Structural Adjustment Attracts World Bank Funds," Middle East Economic Digest 28, no. 38 (21 September 1984): 44.

"Syria's Budget: Where the Cash Flows in '87," The Middle East, (no. 151 (May 1987): 33.)

Tabor, Harry Z. "Using Solar Energy to Desalinate Water," Alternative Futures 28, no. 4, (October-December 1978):

Talling, J. F. "Water Characteristics," Euphrates and Tigris Mesopotamian Ecology and Destiny (The Hague: Dr. W. Junk Monographiae Biologicae, vol. 38, 1980), pp. 63-80.

Taubenblatt, Selig. Presentation made at the Center for Strategic and International Studies Seminar on U.S. Foreign Policy on Water Resources in the Middle East: Instrument for Peace and Development, Washington, D.C., 25 November 1986.

Temko, Ned. "Water: Toughest Issue on the West Bank," Christian Science Monitor, 18 September 1979.

Thornton, J., Some Perspectives on the Potential for Solar Detoxification of Hazardous Wastes,

RI/MR-250-3122 (Golden, Colo.: Solar Energy Research Institute, 1987).

Tleimat, B. W. "Optimal Water Cost from Solar Powered Distillation of Saline Water" Paper presented at the Baghdad Conference, 1-6 December 1981, pp. 459-489.

Tyler, Patrick. "Egyptians Turn to Desert Farming," Washington Post, 24 December 1986, p. 10.

Wallace, John. "Water is Jordan's Top Priority," Middle East Economic Digest 23, no. 12 (23 March 1979): 35.

"Water Politics," The Middle East, special report, no. 76 (February 1981): 47-54.

"Water Power: Who Turns the Tap?" Arab Report, 14 March 1979.

Waterbury, John. Hydropolitics of the Nile Valley (Syracuse, N.Y.:Syracuse University Press, 1979).

_____. "Riverains and Lacustrines: Toward International Cooperation in the Nile Basin," Discussion Paper no. 107 (Princeton, N.J.: Princeton University Research Program in Development Studies, September 1982).

Weihe, H. "Fresh Water from Sea Waters: Distilling by Solar Energy." Solar Energy, 13 (1972): 439-444.

Whittington, D., and G. Guariso. Water Management Models in Practice: A Case Study of the Aswan High Dam (New York: Elsevier Scientific Publishing Co., 1983).

Whittington, D., and K. E. Haynes. "Nile Water for Whom?" Agricultural Development in the Middle East, Peter Beaumont and Keith McLachlan, eds. (New York: John Wiley and Sons, 1985), pp. 125-149.

Wiseman, Boin. "Water Decades Goals Recede as Population Grows," Middle East Economic Digest 26, no. 13 (26 May 1982): 16-18.

World Population Data Sheet (Washington, D.C.: The Population Reference Bureau, Inc., 1986).

Younger, Dana R. "Nonmilitary Water Resources Projects in the Middle East and Horn of Africa: An Overview of the Executive Agencies and the World Bank." Background paper for the Center for Strategic and International Studies Conference on U.S. Foreign Policy on

175

Water Resources in the Middle East and Horn of Africa, Washington, D.C., 20-21 February 1986.

GOVERNMENT DOCUMENTS

Barney, G. O., ed. The Global 2000 Report to the President, vol. 2: The Technical Report. Report prepared for the Council on Environmental Quality and U.S. Department of State, (New York: Pergamon Press, 1980).

Boegli, W. J., M. M. Dahl, and H. E. Remmers. Southwest Region Solar Pond Study for Three Sites: Tularosa Basin, Malaya Bend, and Canadian River. Report prepared for the U.S. Department of the Interior (Denver: GPO, 1984).

Jackson, B., and J. M. Lachowski. "Overview of Pink Water Treatment Tecnology at DARCOM Facilities," U.S. Army Armament Research and Development Center, AS-E401-132 (Dover, N.J.; 1984).

Roth, M., and J. M. Murphy. "Ultraviolet-Ozone and Ultraviolet-Oxidant Treatment of Pink Water," U.S. Army Armament Research and Development Center, ARLLCD-TR-78057 (Dover, N.J.; 1987).

U.S. Department of Commerce, Foreign Economic Trends: Egypt (Washington, D.C.: GPO, 1986).

U.S. Department of Commerce, Foreign Economic Trends: Ethiopia (Washington, D.C.: GPO, 1986).

U.S. Department of Commerce, Foreign Economic Trends: Iraq (Washington, D.C.: GPO, 1986).

U.S. Department of Commerce, Foreign Economic Trends: Israel (Washington, D.C.: GPO, 1986).

U.S. Department of Commerce, Foreign Economic Trends: Jordan (Washington, D.C.: GPO, 1987).

U.S. Department of Commerce, Foreign Economic Trends: Sudan (Washington, D.C.: GPO, 1986).

U.S. Department of Commerce, Foreign Economic Trends: Syria (Washington, D.C.: GPO, 1986).

U.S. Department of Commerce, Foreign Economic Trends: Turkey (Washington, D.C.: GPO, 1985).

U.S. Department of Energy, National Solar Thermal Technology Division, Five Year Research and

Technology Division, Five Year Research and Development Plan, 1986-1990, DOE/CE-0160 (Washington, D.C.: GPO, 1986).

U.S. Department of Energy, Photovoltaic Energy Technology Division, Five Year Research Plan, 1984-1988, Photovoltaics: Electricity from Sunlight, DOE/CE-0072 (Washington, D.C.: GPO, 1983).

U.S. Department of State. Background Notes: Egypt (Washington, D.C.: GPO, 1985).

U.S. Department of State. Background Notes: Ethiopia (Washington, D.C.: GPO, 1985).

U.S. Department of State. Background Notes: Iraq (Washington, D.C.: GPO, 1984).

U.S. Department of State. Background Notes: Israel (Washington, D.C.: GPO, 1984).

U.S. Department of State. Background Notes: Jordan (Washington, D.C.: GPO, 1984).

U.S. Department of State. Background Notes: Sudan (Washington, D.C.: GPO, 1985).

U.S. Department of State. Background Notes: Syria (Washington, D.C.: GPO, 1986).

U.S. Department of State. Background Notes: Turkey (Washington, D.C.: GPO, 1984).

JOINT PUBLICATIONS RESEARCH SERVICE

'Abd al 'Aziz, Faruq, and Jamal Kamal. "Minister of Electricity Warns: We Are at Threshold of Energy Crisis," Al Jumhuriya, 23 January 1986 [NEA-86-043, pp. 5-11].

Basyuni, Muhammed. "Arab Investment Reportedly Increases," Al Majallah, 23 September 1986 [NEA-86-138, pp. 1-4].

Berberoglu, Enis. Cumhuriyet, 3 April 1986 [WER-86-062, pp. 84-85].

Hamid, 'Abda al Wahhab. "Egypt Produces for the First Time, Advanced Agricultural Equipment," Al Ahram: Al Tab'ah Al Duwaliyah, 19 October 1986 [NEA-86-149, 10 December 1986, p. 20].

"How Does Egypt Plan to Confront Food Security Problems," Al Mustaqbal, 11 January 1986 [NEA-86-032, pp. 42-45].

"Investigation of the Reality of Agricultural Crops in Dayr al Zawr," Al Ba'th, 12 June 1986 [NEA-86-109, 4 September 1986, p. 7].

Second Stage," <u>Al Thawrah</u>, 30 June 86.

Al Jubarti, Sayyid, and Hana' Jawhar. "Numerous Employment and Investment Opportunities in New Lands with No One Benefiting," <u>Al Akhbar</u>, 26 October 1986 [NEA-86-151, 12 December 1986, p. 5].

Karakas, Osman. <u>Milliyet</u>, 5 June 1986 [WER-86-088, pp. 98-99].

"Measures to Compensate for Water Shortage with High Dam," <u>Al Ahram: Al Tab'ah al Duwaliyah</u>, 23 October 1986 [NEA-86- 144, pp. 23-24].

Murshid, 'Isa. <u>Al Akhbar</u>, 22 January 1986 [NEA-86-032, p. 48].

Nushi, Fu'ad. "Mr. President, the Parties Have Concluded Their Discussion of the Subsidy Problem," <u>Al Sha'b</u>, 21 October 1986 [NEA-86-154,].

Al Qu'ayd, Yusuf. "Foreign Workers in the Gulf: Competition Between Asians and Egyptians," <u>Al Mustaqbal</u>, 9 August 1986 [NEA-86-139].

Riyad, Sami. <u>Al Ahram</u>, 29 January 1986 [NEA-86-043, p. 30].

Saraya, Usamah. "Egypt's Water Supply Enough to Reclaim One Million Feddans," <u>Al Ahram</u>, 31 January 1986 [NEA-86-038, pp. 49-53].

INTERVIEWS

Al-Anbari, His Excellency Dr. Abdul-Amir. Ambassador of Iraq. Interview with Joyce R. Starr. Washington, D.C., 2 November 1987.

Bell, Robert. Deputy assistant administrator, Bureau for Asia and the Near East, Agency for International Development. Interview with Daniel C. Stoll. Washington, D.C., 22 August 1986.

Ben-Meir, Meir. Director-general of Israeli Ministry of Agriculture. Interview with Joyce R. Starr. Tel Aviv, 15 August 1987.

Berry, Greg. Bureau for Near Eastern and South Asian Affairs, Department of State. Interview with Daniel C. Stoll. Washington, D.C., 21 October 1986.

Buras, Nathan. Head of the Department of Hydrology and Water Resources, University of Arizona. Interview with Daniel C. Stoll. Tuscon, 16

Interview with Daniel C. Stoll. Tuscon, 16 March 1987.

Cleary, Sharon. International environmental officer, Bureau of Oceans and International Environmental and Scientific Affairs, U.S. Department of State. Interview with Daniel C. Stoll. Washington, D.C., 21 October 1986.

Fitzgerald, Worth. Senior water management specialist, Agency for International Development. Interview with Daniel C. Stoll. Washington, D.C., 10 September 1986.

Geary, Frank J. Power engineer, World Bank. Interview with Daniel C. Stoll. Washington, D.C., 15 September 1986.

Hawley, Benjamin. Desk officer, Jordan, Lebanon, and Oman, Agency for International Development. Interview with Daniel C. Stoll. Washington, D.C., 29 October 1986.

Hickox, Robert. Foreign activities specialist, Bureau of Reclamation. Interview with Daniel C. Stoll. Washington, D.C., 8 August 1986.

Holzman, John. Bureau for Near Eastern and South Asian Affairs, U.S. Department of State. Interview with Daniel C. Stoll. Washington, D.C., 19 September 1986.

Ingram, Helen. Professor of political science, University of Arizona. Interview with Daniel C. Stoll. Tuscon, 16 March 1987.

Kerber, Frank. Bureau for Near Eastern and South Asian Affairs, U.S. Department of State. Interview with Daniel C. Stoll. Washington, D.C., 22 October 1986.

Langmaid, Bradshaw. Deputy assistant administrator, Bureau for Science and Technology, Agency for International Development. Interview with Daniel C. Stoll. Washington, D.C., 22 August 1986.

Lintner, Steve. Environmental coordinator, Bureau for Asia and the Near East, Agency for International Development. Interview with Daniel C. Stoll. Washington, D.C., 29 August 1986.

Lord, William. Director of Water Resources Research Center, University of Arizona. Interview with Daniel C. Stoll. Tuscon, 16 March 1987.

Ludan, Robert. Development assistance coordinator,

Bureau for Near Eastern and South Asian Affairs, U.S. Department of State. Interview with Daniel C. Stoll. Washington, D.C., 20 October 1986.

Matlock, W. Gerald. Professor of agricultural engineering, University of Arizona. Interview with Daniel C. Stoll. Tucson, 16 March 1987.

McJunkin, F. Eugene. Environmental engineer, Bureau of Science and Technology, Agency for International Development. Interview with Daniel C. Stoll. Washington, D.C., 2 September 1986.

Moser, C. William. Deputy director, U.S.-Saudi Arabian Joint Economic Commission. Interview with Daniel C. Stoll. Washington, D.C., 19 August 1986.

Moss, Marshall. Assistant chief hydrologist, United States Geological Survey. Interview with Daniel C. Stoll. Washington, D.C., 13 August 1986.

Osborn, Donald. Director of the Solar Energy Facility, University of Arizona. Interview with Daniel C. Stoll. Tuscon, 17 March 1987.

O'Sullivan, Rory. Division chief, World Bank. Interview with Daniel C. Stoll. Washington, D.C., 15 September 1986.

Pommier, Michel J. L. Senior financial analyst, World Bank. Interview with Daniel C. Stoll. Washington, D.C., 24 September 1986.

Porto, Mary. Bureau of Near Eastern and South Asian Affairs, U.S. Department of State. Interview with Daniel C. Stoll. Washington, D.C., 17 September 1986.

Schiff, Ze'ev. Military correspondent, Ha'aretz. Interview with Joyce R. Starr. Tel Aviv, 21 August 1987.

Slack, Donald. Agricultural engineer, University of Arizona. Interview with Daniel C. Stoll. Tuscon, 17 March 1987.

Slater, James. Office of the Under Secretary, Department of the Interior. Interview with Daniel C. Stoll. Washington, D.C., 25 August 1986.

Turner, Barbara. Deputy director, Office of Technical Resources, Bureau for Asia and the Near East, Agency for International Development. Interview with Daniel C. Stoll.

Washington, D.C., 26 August 1986.

Wilson, L. Gray. Hydrologist, University of Arizona. Interview with Daniel C. Stoll. Tuscon, 16 March 1987.

Zelaya, Mario. Sanitary engineer, World Bank. Interview with Daniel C. Stoll. Washington, D.C., 19 September 1986

About the Editors
and Contributors

Ewan W. Anderson is lecturer in the Department of Geography and the Centre for Middle East and Islamic Studies at the University of Durham (England). He has served as advisor to the governments of the United States, Great Britain, and the Sultanate of Oman. He holds a Ph.D. degree in geology and another in education.

Leon Awerbuch is senior business development representative for the Bechtel Group, Inc. A widely recognized expert in water reuse and desalination, he is involved with the operations of the desalination plant in Jeddah, Saudi Arabia--the largest such plant in the world. He is also treasurer of the Board of Directors for the International Desalination Association.

Wayne L. Collins has been associate director of the University of Arizona's Environmental Research Laboratory for sixteen years. He was previously a vice president of Hawaii's Oceanic Foundation, served as the state of Hawaii's first director of Agriculture and Conservation, and during the 1950s and 1960s was a well-known news commentator in Hawaii.

Cem Duna joined the Turkish Ministry of Foreign Affairs in 1969 and has held posts in Saudi Arabia, Great Britain and Holland. He has been counsellor for foreign affairs to Prime Minister Turgut Ozal since 1985.

Carl N. Hodges is the director of the University of Arizona's Environmental Research Laboratory. The laboratory is known for its innovative technology in controlled-environment agriculture and aquaculture; seawater irrigation of plants; and design of the growing exhibit at "The Land," Walt Disney World EPCOT Center. He is currently overseeing the development of a completely closed ecological "biosphere."

Raj Krishna is currently chief counsel at the World Bank for the South Asia region. Before joining the bank's Legal Department in 1969, he taught law at the University of Dehli and Punjab. Dr. Krishna has an extensive publication record on issues related to international law and international economic law.

Medhat Latif, a native of Egypt, is currently a Ph.D. candidate in the Department of Nuclear and Energy Engineering at the University of Arizona. His Master's of Science degree thesis is on the subject of water desalination.

Donald E. Osborn has been director of the University of Arizona's Solar Energy Research Facility since 1981. The facility is responsible for finding interdisciplinary solutions to energy problems. In January 1987, Mr. Osborn was appointed chairman of the Arizona Energy Commission.

James J. Riley is coordinator of International Programs at the University of Arizona's Environmental Research Laboratory. He received his Ph.D. in hydrology at the University of Arizona in 1968. After years in residence in Taiwan and the Sudan, he and his family are now headquartered in the United Arab Emirates.

Raymond Sierka is a professor of civil engineering and engineering mechanics at the University of Arizona. He currently teaches environmental engineering and conducts research on a variety of water treatment techniques including ozone oxidation and advanced water treatment processes.

184

Joyce R. Starr is director for Economic and Social Development Studies and senior fellow for Near East Studies at the Center for Strategic and International Studies. Prior to joining the center in 1979, Dr. Starr served as associate special assistant to the president in the Carter White House.

Daniel C. Stoll has been research associate in the Near East Studies and Council at the Center for Strategic International Studies since 1985.

Selig A. Taubenblatt is presently an executive consultant for Bechtel Financing Services, Inc. He retired from the U.S. government in 1983 after thirty years of public service, which included senior management positions in the Department of State, the U.S. Agency for International Development, and the U.S. Development Loan Fund. From 1977 to 1981, Mr. Taubenblatt had principal responsibility in USAID for the Maqarin Dam negotiations and was also chairman of the State/AID Steering Committee on Jordan River Water Rights. From 1977 to 1983, he was director of project development for the Near East at USAID.

Index

Batinah, 3
Begin, Menachem, 32
Bekaa Valley, 17
Blowdown, 53, 55
Blue Nile basin, 153 See
    also Blue Nile River
Blue Nile River, 14, 15-
    16, 23, 24, 28, 33.
    See also Blue Nile
    basin
Boeing Company, 78
Brown and Root
    International, Inc.,
    119
BSF. See United States,
    -Israel Binational
    Science Foundation
Buraimi, 18
Bureau for Near Eastern
    and South Asian
    Affairs (NEA), 126
Burundi, 24, 31, 32, 34,
    40(table)

Catalytic, Inc., 78
Ceyhan River, 119, 147
Children's Television
    Workshop, 66
Chile, 74
Chlorinated phenols, 84
Chlorination, 120
Congo. See Independent
    State of the Congo
Cyprus, 21(table)

Damascus, 148
Damietta barrage, 25
Dan River, 10, 42
Dan Spring, 7
DBCP. See 1,2-
    dichloro, 3-
    chloropropane
Dead Sea, 7, 144
Defense Intelligence
    Agency (DIA), 132
Dellinger, R., 87
Desalination

of brackish water,
    54, 59, 62(table),
    63(table)
and brine, 70, 80
costs of, 4, 59-60,
    62(table),
    63(table), 65
electrodialysis (ED),
    58-59, 76, 79
multi-effect
    distillation (MED),
    57, 76, 77-78,
    104(fig.)
multistage flash
    (MSF), 55-56
vs. Peace Pipeline,
    121
reverse osmosis (RO),
    58, 76, 79, 81,
    96(table)
of seawater, 54, 55-
    56, 59, 62(table),
    63(table)
and solar energy.
    See desalination,
    solar
and sources of raw
    water, 54-55
status of, 53-54
types of, 54
vapor compression
    (VC), 57-58
See also
    Desalination, solar
Desalination, solar, 4,
    73-79, 135
costs of, 74-75,
    96(table)
and HTME, 81,
    96(table)
See also Desali-
    nation
Detoxification,
    anaerobic-aerobic,
    84
DIA. See Defense
    Intelligence Agency

Donavan, Hamester and
Rattin, Inc., 79
Drought, 2, 37, 149

East African Nile Waters
Coordinating
Committee, 31
East Ghor Canal, 8, 10,
46, 144
ED. See Desalination,
electrodialysis
Edgar, Bob, 88
Egypt, 6, 40(table),
143, 149-150
agriculture of, 14,
29, 116
and Bureau of
Reclamation, 130
Declaration of 1949,
28
drainage systems in,
157
Electrical Authority,
130
and Ethiopia, 133-
134, 154
and Great Britain, 27,
30
Master Water Plan of,
15, 34
Ministry of
Irrigation, 130
and Nile River, 14-17,
24-26, 28-30, 149-
150
population growth of,
150, 162(table)
and SCS, 131
and SOS-7, 116
and Sudan, 16, 24, 25-
26, 28-30
technicians in, 151
and USAID, 127,
138(table)
vegetable oil imports
of, 115
water supply vs.

demand of, 15,
21(table), 34, 150
Eisenhower, Dwight, 9
EPA. See United
States, Environ-
mental Protection
Agency
Ethiopia, 6, 16, 23,
24, 40(table), 149,
153-154
and Egypt, 33-34
famine in, 158
and Nile River, 32,
34, 35
Euhalophytes, 110-111.
See also
Halophytes; SOS-7
Euphrates basin, 11.
See also Euphrates
River; Tigris-
Euphrates basin
Euphrates River, 3, 11,
147
and Iraq, 13, 148-149
mean annual discharge
of, 11, 163(table)
and Syria, 12, 148
and Turkey, 12
See also Tigris-
Euphrates basin
Euphrates River
Authority, 13-14
Evaporation, 11
Exxon, 79
Famine Early Warning
System (FEWS), 157
FAO. See United
Nations, Food and
Agriculture
Organization
FEWS. See Famine Early
Warning System
Floods, 2, 37
Fourth Cataract Dam, 28
France, 5, 26

Ganges River, 133

population of, 49,
    151, 162(table)
raids on East Ghor
    Canal, 10
and solar ponds, 71
and USAID, 139(table)
water consumption in,
    9, 143, 144-145
and West Bank, 8-9,
    153
Italy, 26, 28
Ivekovic, H., 76

Japan, 5
Jebel Awlia Compensation
    Agreement of 1932, 27
Jerusalem, 32
J. G. White Engineering
    Corporation, 33
Johnston, Eric, 9, 44,
    152. See also
    Johnston Plan
Johnston Plan, 10, 44-
47, 152. See also
Johnston, Eric
Jonglei Canal, 16, 31,
    38(n12)
Jordan, 143, 144
  agriculture in, 10, 50
  groundwater resources
    in, 50
  and Iraq, 13
  and Israel, 10, 49,
    153
  and Jordan River, 6-
    7, 43, 152
  Natural Resources
    Authority of, 129
  and Peace Pipeline,
    119, 123(table)
  population of, 49,
    162(table)
  and reprocessed
    sewage, 5
  and SCS, 81
  and Syria, 8, 48, 49,
    144, 145, 153

and United States, 47
and USAID, 127, 128,
    139(table)
and USGS, 141-
    142(table)
Jordan River, 6, 7, 42,
    43, 143, 144, 152,
    163(table). See
    also Jordan River
    basin; Jordan
    Valley
Jordan River basin, 7-
    10, 42-47, 143-144.
    See also Jordan
    River; Jordan
    Valley
Jordan Valley, 42-47,
    144, 146
Jordan Valley
    Authority, 129

Kagera River, 31
Keban Dam, 12
Kenya, 24, 34-35,
    40(table)
Khabur River, 12
Kharun River, 11
Khasm all-Girba
    reservoir, 32
King Talal Dam, 46, 50
Kutch, Gulf of, 115
Kuwait, 5, 53, 120,
    124(table),
    142(table)
Kuwait Institute of
    Scientific
    Research, 4, 77
Kyoga, Lake, 31

Latif, M. G., 74
Lawand, T. A., 74
League of Nations, 33
Lebanon, 1, 6, 17, 43,
    139(table),
    162(table)
Libya, 3, 4, 7,
    21(table)

Litani River, 6, 9, 17

McPherson, M. Peter, 125
Maghreb countries, 1, 6-7
Main Plan, 9
Malta, 5
Maqarin Dam, 8, 47-49, 50, 127. See also Unity Dam; Unity/Maqarin Dam
Maqarin Dam Plan, 47-49
Martin Marietta, 79
MED. See Desalination, multi-effect distillation
Mediterranean-Dead Sea Canal, 8
Morocco, 21(table)
MSF. See Desalination, multistage flash

NASA. See National Aeronautics and Space Administration
Nasser, Gamal Abdel, 25
Nasser, Lake, 16
National Aeronautics and Space Administration (NASA), 158
National Oceanic and Atmospheric Administration (NOAA), 158
National Water Carrier, 8, 46, 144
NEA. See Bureau for Near Eastern and South Asian Affairs
Negev Desert, 17, 46
Niger river Basin Authority, 133
Nile basin, 23, 35-36, 40(table), 149. See also Nile River
Nile Basin Commission, 36-37

Nile River, 3
catchment shared, 6
course of, 23-24, 149
discharge rate, 163(table)
and Egypt, 14-17, 24-26
and Ethiopia, 32, 34
irrigation from, 24
treaties and agreements regarding, 26-31
in Uganda, 23
See also Blue Nile River; Nile basin; White Nile River
Nile Waters Agreement of 1929, 16, 25, 27, 28
Nile Waters Study, 130
NOAA. See National Oceanic and Atmospheric Administration

Office of International Cooperation and Development (OICD), 130-131
OICD. See Office of International Cooperation and Development
Okidi, C. O., 24, 32
Oman, 3, 4, 18, 120, 124(table)
1,2-dichloro, 3-chloropropane (DBCP), 83
1,2,3,4-tetrach-lorobenzene, 108(fig. 5.11)
Orontes River, 6, 12, 17-18
Owen Falls Dam, 25, 28, 31
Ozal, Turgut, 119, 121

Ozone, 82–83,
    105(fig.), 106–
    107(fig.)

Pakistan, 128
Palestinian refugees, 51
Panama Canal Commission,
    133–134
Peace Pipeline, 119–122
  Gulf Pipeline, 120,
    121, 124(table)
  Western Pipeline, 119–
    120, 121, 123(table)
Pesticides, 82, 106–
    107(fig.)
Photo-oxidation, 85–87
Photovoltaics (PVs), 66,
    67–68, 98(fig.)
Pollutants, priority,
    84–85
Population growth, 1,2,
    162(table)
Population Reference
    Bureau, 150
PVs. See Photovoltaics

Qanats, 3
Qatar, 5, 120,
    124(table),
    141(table)
Qatar Solar Energy
    Station, 4
Qirwan, Lake, 17

Rainfall, 1, 19, 43
Republic of Sudan. See
    Sudan
RO. See Desalination,
    reverse osmosis
Roseries Dam, 130
Roseries Reservoir, 28,
    33
Rosetta barrage, 25
Rwanda, 24, 31, 34,
    40(table)

Sadat, Anwar, 32, 33

Salicornia, 112
Saudi Arabia, 3, 11
    desalination projects
    of, 53, 65
    electricity
    generation in, 65
    and Iraqi-Syrian
    dispute, 13
    and Peace Pipeline,
    120, 123(table),
    124(table)
    and Soleras program,
    78
    and Sudan, 17
    and United States,
    129, 134–135
    and USGS, 141–
    142(table)
    Water Atlas of, 129,
    131, 134
Saudi Saline Water
    Conversion
    Cooperation, 135
Saudi Water Atlas, 129,
    131, 134
SCS. See Soil
    Conservation
    Laboratory, 78
Sea of Galilee. See
    Tiberias, Lake
Sea Water Conversion
    Service
SEGS, See Solar Energy
    Generating Station
Sennar Dam, 16, 27, 33
SERI. See Solar Energy
    Research Institute
Sewage, 5, 8, 146–147
Seyhan River, 119, 147
Shatt al-Arab basin, 6.
    See also Shatt al-
    Arab River
Shatt al-Arab River,
    14. See also Shatt
    al-Arab basin
Sinai Desert, 17, 32
Sirte, Gulf of, 4

United Kingdom. See
  Great Britain
United Nations (UN), 147
  Expanded Programme of
    Technical
    Assistance, 31
  Food and Agriculture
    Organization (FAO),
    131
  See also United
    Nations Development
    Program
United Nations Develop-
    ment Program (UNDP),
    31, 33
  Workshop for Nile
    Basin Countries, 35-
    36, 153
United States
  Agency for
    International
    Development. See
    United States Agency
    for International
    Development
  Army Corps of
    Engineers, 132-134
  Bureau of Reclamation,
    33, 80, 81, 130
  Congress, 48
  Department of
    Agriculture (USDA),
    130-131
  Department of Defense,
    132-134
  Department of Energy,
    67-68, 72
  Department of State,
    125-126, 157
  Department of the
    Interior, 129-130
  desalination plants
    of, 53
  Environmental
    Protection Agency
    (EPA), 82, 134
  Geological Survey

(USGS), 129, 141-
    142(table), 158
  interagency
    coordinating body
    for, 158-159
  -Israel Binational
    Agricultural
    Research and
    Development Fund
    (BARD), 132, 135
  -Israel Binational
    Science Foundation
    (BSF), 136
  and Jordan vs.
    Israel, 49
  recommendations for,
    158-160
  -Saudi Arabian Joint
    Commission on
    Economic
    Cooperation, 134-
    135
  solar still
    distillation plants
    in, 95(table)
  and solar thermal
    costs, 102(fig.)
  solar thermal
    techologies in, 71-
    72
  and Soleras program,
    78
  Treasury Department,
    134
  and water crisis,
    154-160
  See also United
    States Agency for
    International
    Development
United States Agency
    for International
    Development
    (USAID), 47, 126-
    128, 138-
    140(table)
  Bureau for Asia and

surface, 21(table), 46
and toxic waste
destruction, 82-88
upstream abstraction
vs. downstream use,
5-6
water crisis, 2, 6,
150-154, 154-160
water tables, 3
Waterbury, John 15, 24,
32, 33, 34, 150,
153
Water for Sanitation and
Health Project
(WASH), 127
Water Resources
Management Action
Group (WARMAG), 132
Water Resources Research
Act, 129-130
Weihe, H., 77
West Bank, 8-9, 49, 51,
139(table), 143, 146
West Bank, The, 146
West Bank Data Project,
146
West Ghor, 42

White Nile River, 14,
11, 23. See also
Blue Nile River;
Nile River
Willcocks, Sir William,
37
World Bank, 34, 131,
148, 150
World Meteorological
Organization, 31
Worldwatch Institute,
143
Worldwide Desalting
Plants Inventory, 54

Yangtze River, 133
Yarmuk River, 7, 8, 10,
42, 43, 48, 50, 144,
145
Yarmuk Triangle. See
Adasiye Triangle
Yevjevich, Vujica, 34

Zaire, 16, 24, 32, 35,
40(table)
Zarqa River, 46
Zor gorge, 42